Nutrition, Sustainable Agriculture and Climate Change in Africa

"This easy-to-read, valuable book provides critical insight into and understanding of the current state of affairs in our agricultural sector as well as a pathway towards achieving a more successful outcome. The book stands out in its discussion of contemporary issues and its concise, yet comprehensive approach."

—Kalama Adefe, *Lecturer, Lancashire School of Business and Enterprise, University of Central Lancashire*

"This well-structured book provides unique insight into and gives an important and informative analysis of the current state of affairs in our agricultural sector."

—Jacob Samuriwo, *Director, Bestfield Consulting*

"The challenges in climate change and sustainable agriculture are both difficult and interesting. However, with the current COVID-19 pandemic and its impact on the economy, it is apparent that academicians and practitioners and working on them with enthusiasm, tenacity, and dedication to develop new methods of analysis and providing working practices and innovative and creative ways pf keeping up with the dynamic pressures and developing policies that would improve the agricultural sector.

This book provides a valuable window into how sustainable agriculture and nutrition security could be accomplished within the context of African countries. With the new era of global interconnectivity and interdependence, practitioners and professionals in the field of study relating to sustainable agriculture, nutrition and climate change would benefit from contemporary knowledge on the frontiers in the industry. As a result, this book is a good step in that direction as it focuses on African perspective."

—Olusoyi Olatokunbo Richard Ashaye, *Housing and Research Consultant, Independent*

Gbadebo Odularu
Editor

Nutrition, Sustainable Agriculture and Climate Change in Africa

Issues and Innovative Strategies

palgrave
macmillan

Editor
Gbadebo Odularu
Department of Economics and Finance
Bay Atlantic University
Washington, DC, USA

ISBN 978-3-030-47874-2 ISBN 978-3-030-47875-9 (eBook)
https://doi.org/10.1007/978-3-030-47875-9

This Palgrave Macmillan imprint is published by the registered company Springer Nature Switzerland AG
The registered company address is: Gewerbestrasse 11, 6330 Cham, Switzerland

Foreword

According to the National Oceanic and Atmospheric Administration, which is part of the U.S. Department of Commerce, the world's five warmest years on record have been its past five. The warming of our planet due to numerous human activities, including agriculture, manufacturing and mining, continues to pose dramatically complex changes to the climate as well as profoundly devastating impact on the global economy to the tune of about 23% reduction in average global incomes by the end of the century. According to the Global Carbon Project, emissions hit a new record of 43.1 billion metric tons in 2019—the third straight year of increases. This trend is likely to continue despite a decline in emissions during the global economic slowdown due to COVID-19. Sustainable agriculture, as an effective solution to potential threat of climate change, focuses on producing climate resilient crops and livestock while having minimal effects on the environment. For decades, most developed countries have produced the bulk of global food through industrial agriculture—a system dominated by large farms growing the same crops year after year, deploying enormous quantities of chemical pesticides and fertilizers that damage the entire ecosystems. However, there is increasingly dire need for Africa to move toward a more socio-economically and environmentally sustainable farming in which diverse range of foods, fibers and fuel production align with agroecological principles. In December 2019, the Socio-Economic Research Applications and Projects (SERAP) Consultants, in collaboration with the Climate Smart Agriculture Youth

Network (CSAYN), co-organized a webinar on "Climate Smart Agriculture as a Means to Creating Decent Jobs for Youth towards Achieving the Agenda 2030 for Sustainable Development". The webinar highlights experiences and share knowledge on how young people around the world are engaging in climate smart agriculture, with particular focus on Africa. In addition, SERAP LLC is committed to providing knowledge and networking support to African countries to leveraging nutrition security and sustainable agriculture strategies for ameliorating the adverse impact of the changing climate on vulnerable communities in Africa and other developing countries.

Sebnem Sahin, Ph.D.
Lead, Development Economist—Free Lancer
IFPRI, World Bank and the OECD
President and Founder, SERAP LLC
Socio-Economic Research Applications & Projects LLC
http://www.serapllc.com
Advisor, Infinite-Sum Modeling Inc.
http://infisum.com/index.php/2018/08/07/sebnem-sahin/
Adjunct Professor, Bay Atlantic University, Washington, DC
https://www.bau.edu/faculty/

Sebnem Sahin is the United Nations Development Program (UNDP)—Sustainable Development Goals (SDGs) Platform Project Lead Modeling Specialist. She is a development economist with more than 15 years' experience. Following her Ph.D. at the Sorbonne University, she deepened her expertise in economic modeling during her career at international development institutions such as the UNDP, World Bank, OECD, and IFPRI. Her assignments include a variety of energy related topics such as economy-wide impacts of removal of electricity subsidies in developing countries, energy-water nexus in South Asia, economic analysis of conflict in oil exporting economies, etc. She was the Task Team Leader for the World Bank report entitled "Low Water-High Growth in South Asia" that was recognized by donors and academia globally. Dr. Sahin is also the Founder and President of the SERAP (Socio-Economic Research Applications and Projects) LLC, an economic research consultancy based in Washington DC.

Acknowledgments

Our deep gratitude goes to God Almighty who is the source of known and future frontiers of intelligence, knowledge, and wisdom. God Almighty has been the only source of courage, energy, strength, and direction through this and other endeavors. Many thanks to every author who contributed to this book, many of whom are leading authorities in their fields. The collaborative efforts of all the authors resulted in the successful finalization of this book. In addition, this publication has benefited immensely from the editor's robust career experience gathered from reputable organizations such as the United States Department of Agriculture, Center for the Study of the Economies of Africa (CSEA), Bay Atlantic University (BAU), Socio-Economic Research Applications and Projects (SERAP), Old Dominion University (ODU), World Trade Organization (WTO), United Nations Economic Commission for Africa (UNECA), United Nations Institute for Development Economic Planning (UNIDEP), International Food Policy Research Institute (IFPRI), Trade Policy Training Center in Africa (TRAPCA), Trade Policy Research and Training Program (TPRTP), University of Ibadan, University of Sunderland, Covenant University, the Forum for Agricultural Research in Africa (FARA), and the African Finance and Economics Association (AFEA).

Significant appreciation is expressed to our spouses, partners, children, parents, colleagues, friends, and others for the provision of an enabling environment during the book project implementation. I say thank you to Professor Sebnem Sahin, who is the Founder and President of the Socio-Economic Research Applications and Projects (SERAP LLC), for her foresightedness and leadership in advocating for the adoption of out-of-the-box approaches in tackling sustainable development challenges. Lastly, we (the editor, authors, and contributors) gratefully acknowledge the support and cooperation provided by Elizabeth Graber, Sophia Siegler, Susan Westendorf and the entire Economics Acquisition Team at Palgrave Macmillan, United States. We also thank countless others who have supported in the finalization of this book project.

Contents

About the Editor

Gbadebo Odularu teaches Economics at Bay Atlantic University, Washington, DC. He is the Trade and Digitization Research and Practice Leader at Socio-Economic Research Applications & Projects (SERAP LLC), Washington, DC. In addition to being a Non-Resident Fellow (NRF) at the Centre for the Study of the Economies of Africa (CSEA), Nigeria, Odularu is affiliated with the Center for Research on Political Economy (CREPOL), Senegal, Old Dominion University, Virginia, as well as the American Heritage University of Southern California (AHUSC). He works closely with national, continental and international partners to provide evidence-based policy tools for fostering sustainable agriculture and digital economy towards realizing the United Nations Sustainable Development Goals (UN SDGs) 2030. One of his most recent books is *Strategic Policy Options for Bracing Nigeria for the Future of Trade* (Palgrave Macmillan, 2020).

Notes on Contributors

Samuel Sesan Abolarin is a Ph.D. student at the University of Agriculture, Makurdi, Benue State, Nigeria. He is a season teacher, has taught in many secondary schools in Katsina State and rose to the position of Principal, he has also served as an independent facilitator with Deloitte Nigeria and he has served as an ad-hoc staff to UNICEF Katsina and Kano field office on Nutrition. He is currently on research. His research interests are Agricultural Policy, Development Economics, Agricultural value chain, and Agricultural Finance. Samuel Sesan Abolarin has published many articles in reputed local and international Journal and conference proceedings. He loves listening to gospel music, politics, travelling, and watching football, etc. He is happily married with children.

Adebola Adedugbe serves as the lead partner at Farmideas Nigeria. His previous and current professional works have consistently focused on Agriculture, Climate Change, Agribusiness, Youth and Women empowerment, Value addition, and Rural Development issues. He has intensively interacted with farmers, stakeholders, and scientists from various disciplines and cultural backgrounds. He engages, mobilizes, and trains young men and women on entrepreneurship especially along the agricultural value chain. He has also been privileged to attend and speak at some major international meetings within and outside Nigeria. He holds a degree in Economics and Certificates in agriculture related courses. He is a member of the Young Professionals in Agricultural Development (YPARD) and served as the local Rep for the FCT Abuja and Nasarawa State in Nigeria between 2015–2016. He belongs to several professional bodies and lives in Abuja, Nigeria where the operational head of his initiative is situated.

Folasade Adegboye is a Lecturer, Department of Banking and Finance, Covenant University, Ota, Nigeria, with research interest in International Finance, Foreign Direct Investment/Aids, and Economic Development. She had a first degree in Accounting, second degree in Finance, and third degree in Banking and Finance. She is an Associate of the Chartered Institute of Banker of Nigeria. She has attended and presented papers in both international and local conferences/workshops.

Bamidele Adekunle is affiliated with the School of Environmental Design and Rural Development, University of Guelph. He also teaches at the Ted Rogers School of Management, Ryerson University, Canada. He was an Adjunct Professor (2013–2016) in the Urban and Inner City Studies program of the University of Winnipeg while working on Manitoba Research Alliance/Social Sciences and Humanities Research Council of Canada (SSHRC) project on inner city Winnipeg. He is a resource person for the African Economic Research Consortium (AERC) and has presented several papers at the Trade Policy Training Center in Africa (TRAPCA). His research interests are in entrepreneurship, financial and institutional economics, agricultural economics, small business and rural development, environmental management, ethnocultural analytics, and international trade. He holds a B.Agric. (Agricultural Economics), M.Sc. (Agricultural Economics), M.B.A. (General Management), and Ph.D. (Agricultural Economics and Business).

Monica Akokuwebe has a Ph.D. degree in Sociology (with Demography and Population Studies as specialization) from the University of Ibadan (Nigeria). She was a former Postdoctoral Fellow in the Demography and Population Studies Program at the University of the Witwatersrand (South Africa), and a recipient of URC Postdoctoral Fellowships, South Africa; the National Research Foundation, South Africa; the DST-NRF Center of Excellence in Human Development, South Africa; the William and Flora Hewlett Foundation; and the National Institute for the Humanities and Social Sciences Funding for Research, South Africa (Grant no. A0060498). She has supervised, examined, and taught at the undergraduate and postgraduate levels. She has over 20 publications in ISI and IBSS accredited journals and book chapters. Her research interests are in the fields of Sociology, Demography, and Population Studies.

She is currently working on a research project titled: "Determinants and Levels of Cervical Cancer Screening Uptake among Women of Reproductive Age in South Africa: evidence from South Africa Demographic and Health Survey Data, 2016."

Ayuba Ali is a Lecturer in the Department of Agricultural Economics, Federal University of Agriculture Makurdi, Nigeria. He obtained B.Agric. (Agricultural Economics and extension, 2007), M.Sc. in Agricultural Economics (2015) and currently running his Doctor of Philosophy (Ph.D.) in Agricultural Economics at the University of Federal University of Agriculture Makurdi, Nigeria. The author being young in the profession has contributed some articles in academic journals of national and international repute. His research interests focus on marketing, production economics, and agricultural policy and development. He is single.

Olatokunbo Akinseye Aluko is the Principal consultant of Bestfield Business and Management Consultants, UK. This is a world-class consultancy organization with strategic alliances across the world. Dr. Akinseye Olatokunbo Aluko is the Deputy Program Leader/Lecturer in Oil & Gas Management & International Strategic Management, respectively, at the University of East London (UEL). He started his lecturing career at the University of Teesside, Middlesbrough where he got his M.Sc. in International Management and an M.B.A. in Business Administration, respectively. And he later lectured at the University of Sunderland where he later got his Ph.D. in "Strategic Change Management in the Maritime Crude Oil Transportation in Nigeria." He has also lectured at some prestigious UK Universities/Colleges such as; Teesside University, UWS, Northumbria University, London School of Business and Finance, Manchester Campus, UK College of Business and Computing, London, London School of Science and Technology and to mention a few. His areas of research interest are Sustainability & Transition in Oil & Gas Management, Strategic Change Management, Strategic Entrepreneurship, Maritime Crude Oil Transportation, Strategic Mobility, Strategic Marketing and to mention a few. Dr. Aluko has also held the positions of a marketing manager and logistics and operation manager, respectively; where he identified and managed relationships with large oil & gas and shipping companies for the distribution of petroleum products and shipping maritime facilities, using contextual widgets and site sections. He' also accustomed to successfully juggling multiple projects and has an excellent track record of building new businesses, forging strong relationships with clients, developing partnerships, and increasing company revenue through innovative and creative strategies. Recently, Dr. Aluko became a Fellow of the Chartered Management Institute (FCMI) due to his academic and research achievements in International Strategic Management.

Celina Biam is the current Dean of Agricultural Economics and Extension, University of Agriculture, Makurdi, Benue State, Nigeria. She obtained her Ph.D. from Ebonyi State University, Ebonyi State. She is the author of several articles published in reputed international journals and conference proceedings. She is happily married with children.

Aye Goodness Chioma is an Associate Professor and currently the Head of Department of Agricultural Economics, University of Agriculture, Makurdi-Nigeria. She has obtained several research grants and supervised several undergraduate and postgraduate students. She has authored in several articles and conferences proceedings at both national and international levels. Her research interest includes agricultural policy and planning, production economics, agricultural finance, times series analysis.

Mariama Deen-Swarray is a research manager at the BBC Media Action and a research associate with Research ICT Africa (RIA). Mariama has over 10 years of experience working in Research and mainly in the ICT sector. Mariama has worked extensively on data analysis and conducted both quantitative and qualitative studies and has experience in evidence-based demand-side and supply-side ICT research and ICT policy analysis. Her interest is in gender-related issues in addressing digital inequality. Mariama worked as Head of Research & Studies at ITASCAP, a private financial services and research institution in Sierra Leone and as a researcher at the Namibian Economic Policy Research Unit (NEPRU) in Namibia. She has been involved in the information and communication technology sector and has worked in several ICT related studies. She has participated in ICT Conferences and has contributed to several publications in the field of ICT. Mariama holds a Masters (M.Phil.) in Economics from the University of Ghana and a B.Sc. (First Class) in Computer Science and Economics from the University of Namibia.

Donald Denen Dzever is a Lecturer in the Department of Agricultural Economics, Federal University of Agriculture Makurdi, Nigeria. He obtained a Master of Science (M.Sc.) in Agricultural Economics from the Federal University of Agriculture, Makurdi. He is currently pursuing his Doctor of Philosophy (Ph.D.) in Agricultural Economics at the same University. He is currently an examination officer at the Department of Agricultural Economics and has authored several articles in reputable journals and conference proceedings. He has supervised many undergraduate students and his research interest includes production economics, agricultural policy, and development as well as resource and environmental economics.

Oben Njock Emmanuel is a monitoring and evaluation officer for mission 21 and instructor in the Department of Agricultural Economics and Agribusiness, University of Buea, Cameroon. He completed his Master of Science (M.Sc.) in Agribusiness at the University of Agriculture, Makurdi-Nigeria. He is presently a Doctor of Philosophy (Ph.D.) aspirant in Agricultural Economics and Agribusiness at the University of Buea. He has published a research paper. His research interest includes agribusiness management, agricultural marketing, production economics, agricultural finance and management.

Djomo Choumbou Raoul Fani is a Lecturer in the Department of Agricultural Economics and Agribusiness, Faculty of Agriculture and Veterinary Medicine, University of Buea, Cameroon. He completed his Doctor of Philosophy (Ph.D.) in Agricultural Economics at the University of Agriculture, Makurdi-Nigeria. His international experience includes a research fellowship with International Institute of Tropical Agriculture (IITA) under the project "Youth Researching Youth: Competitive Fellowships for Young African Scholars Researching Youth Engagement in Rural Economic Activities in Africa and, inception and capacity building training for the African Economic Research Consortium (AERC) Collaborative Research Project on Impact of Agricultural and Food Policies on Nutrition Outcomes in Africa (AFPON) Project-Country Case Studies Phase." He can also look back to 14 years' experience in consultancy for development projects where he focused on monitoring and evaluation, impact assessment, teaching, training, and capacity building activities. He has authored several articles in peer review journals: book chapters and conferences proceedings at both national and international levels. His research collaboration includes among others and not limited to the Federal University of Agriculture, Makurdi-Nigeria; Federal University Wukari-Nigeria, International Institute of Tropical Agriculture (IITA), Ibadan-Nigeria; North-West University, South Africa; Bay Atlantic University,

Washington-USA; Michigan State University, USA; University of Gothenburg, Sweden. His research interests center on production economics, farm management, agricultural policy and development, agricultural finance, environmental economics, system dynamics modeling approach in agriculture, development economics, climate change analysis.

Ogebe Frank is a senior lecturer in the Department of Agricultural Economics, University of Agriculture, Makurdi-Nigeria. He has authored in several articles and conferences proceedings at both national and international levels. He has supervised several undergraduate students. His research interest includes health economics, production economics, farm management, agricultural finance.

Ukpe Udeme Henrietta is a senior lecturer in the Department of Agricultural Economics and Extension, Federal University Wukari, Nigeria. She completed her Doctor of Philosophy (Ph.D.) in Agricultural Economics at the University of Agriculture, Makurdi-Nigeria. She is currently a departmental coordinator for student industrial work experience schemes. She has authored in several articles and conferences proceedings at both national and international levels. She has supervised many undergraduate students and her research interest includes production economics, agricultural policy and development, agricultural finance, environmental economics, development economics, climate change, agricultural marketing.

Oluwatoyin Matthew is an astute Researcher and a Senior Lecturer, Department of Economics and Development Studies, Covenant University, Ota, Nigeria. She holds both first and postgraduate degrees in Economics. She has many years of work experience in teaching at the high school and University levels and published vastly in reputable local and international Scopus indexed journals and attended several international conferences and workshops.

Priscilla Monyai is a Professor and the Head of Department of Development Studies, as well as the Deputy Dean, Faculty of Management and Commerce, University of Fort Hare, South Africa. She is widely published in international and peer-reviewed scholarly journals.

Ndakasharwa Muchaonyerwa holds a Ph.D. degree in Library Information Science from the University of KwaZulu Natal, Durban, South Africa. She specializes in Knowledge Management. She is currently a

Senior Lecturer and Head of Department, Library and Information Science, Faculty of Social Science and Humanities, University of Fort Hare, Alice Campus, Eastern Cape, South Africa. She has published in many internal journals of repute.

Ngo Valery Ngo is a medical doctor and a trained Global Health physician at the postgraduate level. He graduated from Ahmadu Bello University teaching hospital (ABUTH), Shika, Zaria, Kaduna, Kaduna State, Nigeria with Bachelor of Medicine, Bachelor of Surgery (MBBS). After five years of active clinical practice at the Federal Medical Center and innovative Biotech, Keffi, Nasarawa State, Nigeria. He proceeded to study Global Health at the School of Public Health and Community Medicine, the Sahlgrenska Academy, University of Gothenburg, Sweden. His research interest includes global health, global governance, biostatistics, qualitative methods, vaccination, malnutrition, conflicts, emergency preparedness, disaster management, antimicrobial resistance, climate change, health economics, maternal and child health.

Ugochukwu Christopher Nnama is a lecturer in the Department of Agricultural Economics, Federal University of Agriculture Makurdi, Nigeria. He has obtained the Bachelor of Agriculture (B.Agric.) degree in Agricultural Economics and Extension (second class Upper) and Master of Science (M.Sc.) in Agricultural Economics from the Federal University of Agriculture Makurdi, Benue State Nigeria and the Federal University of Technology Owerri, Imo State Nigeria respectively. He is currently pursuing his Doctor of Philosophy (Ph.D.) in Agricultural Economics at the University of Nigeria Nsukka. He currently teaches Agricultural Production Economics and Development at undergraduate levels. His research interests includes; Agricultural Marketing, Trade and Value Chain Analysis. He has over 10 years of teaching and research experience. Mr. Ugochukwu is happily married with a son.

Adenike Odularu is currently the Federal Ministry of Industry, Trade and Investment (FMITI) Chief Commercial Officer. She was one of the 2012–2017 Nigeria-domiciled World Bank Growth and Employment (GEM) project supervisors and Project Management Unit (PMU) members. She is also one of the committee members on Nigeria's ratification of the WTO Trade Facilitation Agreement.

Olufunmilayo Odularu holds a Bachelors and Masters degrees in Geography from the University of Ibadan (U.I.), Nigeria. She also has a second

Masters degree in Development Studies from the University of Fort Hare, South Africa. She is currently a doctoral student at the University of Fort Hare, South Africa.

Oluwayemi IbukunOluwa Olatoye holds a Masters and Ph.D. degree in Library Information Science from Nigeria's Premier University, i.e., the University of Ibadan, Ibadan, Nigeria and the University of Fort Hare, Alice, South Africa, respectively. She specializes in Knowledge Management, Information Security and ICT literacy skills. She is currently a Postdoctoral Fellow at the Department of Library and Information Science, Faculty of Social Science and Humanities, University of Fort Hare, Alice Campus, Eastern Cape, South Africa. Dr. Oluwayemi Olatoye has presented research papers in many international conferences and published in several international journals.

Tolulope Ayodeji Olatoye holds two Masters and Ph.D. degrees in Geographical Information Systems and Environmental Geography from Nigeria's Premier University, i.e., the University of Ibadan, Ibadan, Nigeria and the University of Fort Hare, Alice, South Africa, respectively. He specializes in Environmental Geography, Forest Ecology, Urban Studies, GIS, and Climate Change research. He is currently a Principal Research Fellow at Forestry Research Institute of Nigeria, Jericho, Ibadan, Nigeria. Dr. Tolulope Olatoye has presented over 25 research papers in international conferences and published in many international journals of repute.

Romanus Osabohien is a Ph.D. student, an Assistant Lecturer in the Department of Economics and Development Studies, a Research Associated at the Center for Economic Policy and Development Research (CEPDeR), Covenant University, Ota, Nigeria. His main research focus is on Agricultural and Development Economics. He has attended and presented research papers in international conferences/workshops and has published peer-reviewed papers in rated journals.

Joseph Chinedu Umeh is a Professor of Agricultural Economics at University of Agriculture, Makurdi, Benue State, Nigeria. Professor Umeh received his B.Sc., M.Sc., and Doctoral degrees in Agricultural Economics from the University of Ibadan, Ibadan, Nigeria. His research interests are in the area of Production Economics, Quantitative Techniques, Development Economics, and Health Economics. Professor Umeh's primary responsibility is teaching and research. He has therefore taught undergraduate and postgraduate students and carried out several researches, an activity he enjoys very much. Umeh has production Economics and other related subjects in some other discipline like Economics, Engineering (Economics for Engineering), Business Administration (Managerial Economics), etc. Professor Umeh has published many research papers and books in both local and international research outlets. He has also consulted for a number of local and international organizations, FAO inclusive. Professor Umeh has been an external examiner to large number of Universities and a visiting professor to a good number of Department of Agricultural Economics and Economics. In 1992 and 2012 he was elected Dean of Agricultural Economics and Extension. He loves listening to Christian music, reading current affairs, watching football, etc. He is happily married with children.

List of Figures

List of Tables

CHAPTER 1

Introduction: Nutrition, Sustainable Agriculture and Climate Change Issues in Africa

Mariama Deen-Swarray, Gbadebo Odularu, and Bamidele Adekunle

Introduction: Nutrition, Sustainable Agriculture and Development Issues

According to the United States Department of Agriculture (USDA), nutritional security refers to 'a situation that exists when all people, at all times, have physical, social and economic access to sufficient safe,

M. Deen-Swarray
Research ICT Africa (RIA), Cape Town, South Africa

BBC Media Action, Freetown, Sierra Leone

G. Odularu (✉)
Department of Economics and Finance, Bay Atlantic University, Washington, DC, USA

B. Adekunle
School of Environmental Design and Rural Development, University of Guelph, Guelph, ON, Canada

G. Odularu (ed.), *Nutrition, Sustainable Agriculture and Climate Change in Africa*,
https://doi.org/10.1007/978-3-030-47875-9_1

and nutritious foods that meets their dietary needs and food preferences for an active and healthy life.' In Sub-Saharan Africa (SSA), increasing population growth and expanding demand for agricultural commodities are consistently mounting pressure on land and water resources, thereby posing huge challenges on the region's capacity to achieve nutritional security related to United Nations Sustainable Development Goals (SDGs), especially SDGs 2 and 4. Although SSA boasts of vast, fertile and uncultivated arable lands, its capacity to contribute to feeding its current and future population is seriously being undermined by factors such as low or poor adoption and utilization of innovations and digital tools, impact of climate change, environmental degradation, weak political will, limited interest in farming, lack of government support, etc. However, and in spite of these constraints, sustainable agriculture, food and nutrition security in SSA can be achieved by adopting a multipronged approach, which includes improved agricultural mechanization, adoption of high yielding crop varieties, market access, use of ICT, digital tools, GIS, public investments to facilitate access to improved technologies, provision of rural infrastructure, etc. The purpose of this book is to provide innovative policy tools for enhancing SSA's capacity to achieve sustainable agriculture, food and nutrition security in this digital age and in the face of climate variability. In addition, this book will present some smart strategies for increased production, reduced food wastes as well as enhanced nutritional outcomes through transformative discoveries in agricultural research, education and advisory or extension services.

Despite its wealth of natural resources, youthful population and emerging technological base, it is seemingly unthinkable that Africa currently holds over 60% of the remaining arable land on earth, while it spends billions of its scarce foreign exchange earnings. In other words, and with limited strategic food reserves in the face of natural calamities such as flooding, epidemics and droughts, many African countries rely heavily on food imports to feed its citizens (World Bank 2020). According to Abrams and Smedley (2020), for every US$1 billion that Africa spends on food imports is equivalent to its annual income of 334,000 farming households, which invariably represents 670,000 on-farm jobs and 200,000 off-farm jobs. This Africa's food import situation shows the unsustainability characteristics of its agri-food systems. One lesson to be learnt as Africa strives to manage its post-COVID-19 economies is the need for a more pro-poor, resilient and sustainable agri-food systems, which include its supply chains, markets, infrastructure and capacities to respond proactively to future exogenous shocks in the post-COVID-19 world.

Every year, millions of children and mothers die and suffer from both physical and mental impairment due to poor nutrition during a critical 1000-day period (Child Health 2020). Based on the global food and nutrition security (FNS) metrics, one out of every three persons are undernourished, overweight or obese; one in five children under five (or approximately 161 million) are stunted; and many countries lose some of their GDP due to undernutrition—up to 11% in the hardest-hit African and Asian countries (Brookings 2017). Relating this to undernutrition at the global level, in 2016, 155 million children under five were estimated to be stunted (too short for age), 52 million were estimated to be wasted (too thin for height), 41 million were overweight or obese and 45% of child deaths are associated with undernutrition (UNICEF 2017). This ongoing global dynamic has resulted in increasingly renewed focus on the need to make agricultural policies more 'nutrition-sensitive' (FAO/IFAD/UNICEF/WFP/WHO 2017; BMGF 2012; FAO 2012). However, civilization, changing culture, technology and global land investment dynamics are creating markets for land, thereby influencing the land access—nutrition outcomes relations at communal, national, continental and international levels.

In April 2016, the UN General Assembly endorsed the outcome documents of the Second International Conference on Nutrition (ICN2), aimed at achieving the global nutrition targets set by the World Health Assembly, and declared the period 2016–2025 as the United Nations Decade of Action on Nutrition. The primary objective of the Decade of Action on Nutrition is to increase nutrition investment and implement policies and programmes to improve food security and nutrition within the ICN2 framework[1] (FAO/IFAD/UNICEF/WFP/WHO 2017[2]; FAO/WHO 2013; Herforth et al. 2012). For Africa, the

[1] FAO/WHO Work Programme of the UN Decade of Action on Nutrition (2016–2025). The Decade of Action on Nutrition provides an opportunity for all partners to work together, mobilize action and accelerate efforts towards eliminating hunger, food insecurity and all forms of malnutrition, meeting the SDGs by 2030.

[2] The 2017 State of Food Security and Nutrition in the World (SOFI) Report marks the beginning of the new era in consistent monitoring of progress made towards achieving the food security and nutrition targets set by the United Nations Sustainable Development Goals (UN SDGs) 2030 Agenda, with specific focus on ending hunger (SDG Target 2.1) and all forms of malnutrition (SDG Target 2.2). This coincides with the launch

Comprehensive Africa Agriculture Development Programme (CAADP) shows that the prevalence of undernourishment, underweight, stunting and wasting in children under five years of age have all decreased since the launch of CAADP in 2003, although rather slowly (Jones et al. 2010; Covic and Hendricks 2016; Sahn and Younger 2017).

African poor small farm holders are dependent on land in order to access credit and related input resources. However, securing access to arable productive land has been on a declining trend as a result of the pressure of teeming population, worsening land degradation due to changing climate and more importantly land grabbing (FAO 2010). From a gender perspective, when women are self-employed as farmers, they generate limited incomes because they do not have rights to own or inherit land and to access input or credit markets. Further, land grabbing influence nutrition outcomes, vis-a-vis the different roles and responsibilities of men and women in securing adequate food and nutrition at the household level (Dumas et al. 2018; Owusu et al. 2016; Menon et al. 2014; Vogl 2007). This shifting gender roles due to land ownership dynamics can affect household welfare where women access to productive resources, especially land, may influence children's nutrition (Allendorf 2007; Galiani and Schargrodsky 2004). In view of this, the Bill and Melinda Gates Foundation (BMGF)'s actionable impact objective on nutrition 'ensures that all women and children have the nutrition they need to live healthy and productive lives.'

Rationale, Expected Contribution to Knowledge and the Value Add

Over time, nutrition has been a neglected area of global public health, accounting for less than one per cent of the global development aid largely due to its over-hidden contribution to child illness and deaths (Child Health 2020). At the SSA level, this is also evident in the fact that its food and nutrition landscape is characterized by hunger (undernourishment, micronutrient deficiencies, stunting and child mortality), inadequate food consumption, food insecurity and volatile food prices, thereby posing as a huge impediment to socioeconomic and sustainable development.

of the United Nations Decade of Action of Nutrition (2016–2025), adding impetus to these nutrition-related commitments from a broadened perspectives and multi-partnership platform which comprises global actors such FAO, IFAD, WHO, UNICEF and WFP.

This is evident in a vicious cycle of underdevelopment in which poor communities consist of unhealthy inhabitants with high rates of illness and disability, and whose health systems are inefficient, thereby lacking the adequate capacity to deal with complicated nutrition challenges or preventing them from happening in the first place.

In recent years, access to resources, mainly land, markets and institutions have been, and will continue to be subject to tremendous pressure with both positive and negative implications for agricultural development and food security and nutrition (FSN) in Africa. Consequently, much debate has been raised on whether foreign direct investment in land property and institutions is inimical or beneficial for agricultural development in Africa. However, there ongoing discussion on philosophical paradigms policies and management techniques to ameliorate the risks and therefore, optimize on the workable land policy reform opportunities, as well as on the significant role being played by local governments in strengthening land institutions and adapting climate smart agriculture practices in Africa.

Furthermore, an advanced understanding of climate change policies and nutrition pathways should help improve CSA policy development and programme design for improved nutrition outcomes in SSA. Nutrition outcomes can be enhanced by all community partners—general education, Health, Dental Health, Nutrition, Education, Family Services, Disabilities and Mental Health. In addition, Governments, the United Nations, FAO, IFAD, UNICEF, WFP, WHO, BMGF, bilateral organizations, Alive & Thrive, Helen Keller international, HarvestPlus,[3] Global Alliance for Improved Nutrition, notable universities and the private sector can collaborate towards developing, testing, and rolling out innovative solutions and addressing the obstacles to effective implementation, particularly barriers to reaching women and girls and addressing social and gender norms. In spite of all these efforts and in the face of emerging research over the past few decades, global knowledge about the immediate and underlying causes of undernutrition remains minimal and incomplete, while this same challenge becomes increasingly precarious for SSA with particular focus on fragile countries like politically tensed Cameroon and post-civil war (and post-Ebola) Sierra Leone. Thus,

[3] HarvestPlus support countries globally to test and release biofortified nutritious crops so that farmers and consumers can enjoy the benefits of these crops—Beans, Cassava, Maize, Pearl Millet, Rice, Wheat and Orange Sweet Potato.

the purpose of this book aligns with the BMGF's strategy which focuses on developing new tools and platforms to enable timely collection and analysis of data; supporting global efforts to standardize the collection and monitoring of nutrition data; and use evidence to develop effective policies and guidelines towards combating malnutrition, land degradation, climate variability and socioeconomic shocks like the COVID-19 pandemic.

Over the past decade, there has been an increasing need for the adoption of innovative tools, evidence-based research and novel solutions towards scaling up/out nutrition and CSA interventions. According to the BMGF, fully scaling up current interventions would address only about half of the burden of malnutrition because of its complex causes. Against the background that quite a few studies have been undertaken to examine land property rights, climate unpredictability and nutrition outcomes nexus in SSA, this book will build on earlier research attempts to further our understanding of sustainable agriculture and climate smart pathways in addressing mal- and undernutrition challenges in these SSA countries. In addition to discussing the pros and cons of climate changeability, land-related FDI, this book will also collect the most recent data to identify new issues, as well as look at the available evidence and case studies that discuss the relationship between land ownership and selected measurements of undernutrition in West and Central Africa. Thus, the research will discuss how sustainable agriculture policy, especially for agriculture (and for women) has evolved over the past four decades in the region. This research will also capture some of the contemporary policy-oriented nutrition research, with the aim of documenting recent findings and developing new solutions. As a follow-up to other recent work on the impact of agricultural development interventions on children nutrition outcomes (Dumas et al. 2018; Owusu et al. 2016), this study will generate relevant and most updated information for updating and developing appropriate gender-sensitive policies on climate change and nutrition relations. In other words, this study will provide more understanding on the full range of issues on the climate change—nutrition outcomes nexus, as well as recommend evidence-based policy interventions. This will strengthen the level of existing knowledge by producing and delivering a new body of evidence and narrative that are geared towards policymakers' needs on what works and what does not work, thereby deepening capacity for nutrition-informed policymaking in selected West and Central African countries.

Based on the seemingly inadequate amount of studies and documentation on the role of ineffective land property rights in influencing nutrition outcomes, this research will be leveraging on the combination of mainstream and out-of-the box thinking to generate more novel ideas on the impact of land rights on strategically selected nutrition outcomes—undernourishment, micronutrient deficiencies, stunting, etc. As one of the value added of this study, it is expected that some of the outcomes of the study will propose effective policies that could address the underlying contribution of gender inequality to the land rights—malnutrition dynamics, placing particular emphasis on women's economic and social empowerment, and through that promoting nutrition outcome (Dumas et al. 2018; Owusu et al. 2016; Allendorf 2007; Galiani and Schargrodsky 2004).

Due to high dependence and monetary/cultural attachment to land and agriculture as the main sources of livelihood, women face more severe constraints in accessing land, markets and other factors of production when compared with their men counterparts. Thus, the roles of women cannot be overemphasized in promoting improved nutrition outcomes through nutrition-sensitive land reforms and Climate Smart Agriculture (CSA) interventions (Menon et al. 2014; Allendorf 2007).

This book will fill the yawning nutrition-specific policy gap by demonstrating an association between climate change and nutrition outcomes, while placing emphasis for the role of gender, as well as production of targeted nutrition-rich crops, homestead gardens and diversification of agricultural production systems towards fresh fruits, vegetables, spices and related horticultural crops.

Objective

In recent years, access to resources, mainly land markets and institutions have been, and continue to be, subject to tremendous pressure with both positive and negative implications for agricultural development and food security and nutrition (FSN) in Africa. Consequently, much debate has been raised on whether foreign direct investment in land property and institutions is inimical or beneficial for FNS, and agricultural development in Africa.

The broad objective of this book is to discuss the relevant and current policy issues aimed at enhancing nutrition outcomes and sustainable agriculture within changing climatic and environmental scenarios in Africa. Specifically, this study will:

- Understand the political economy of nutrition security, sustainable agriculture and climate change in Africa.
- Review the relevant literature towards expatiating on the factors that drive nutritional outcomes in the region.
- Based on these findings and lessons generated thereof, evidence-based policy recommendations will be articulated for dissemination to the relevant policy makers, non-government organizations and stakeholders.

The Flow and Organization of Chapters

This book provides a comprehensive analysis on the relationship between nutrition, health, climate change, environment, agriculture and sustainable development, with a special interest in sustainably enhancing Africa's nutritional outlook in the post COVID-19 pandemic era. It examines the contributions of nutrition, community development and agricultural transformation-related policies, programmes, tools and initiatives in the face of changing climate and agribusiness ecosystem. The authors recommend innovative conceptual frameworks, appropriate initiatives and workable policy nuggets towards realizing continental nutritional agenda within a climate-smart agricultural topography.

This book comprises twelve chapters. The book chapters present compelling discussions on the opportunities to improve nutrition and sustainable agricultural development policy processes in Africa. As a follow-up to this introductory chapter, the second chapter of this book discusses how crop and livestock production respond to rainfall and temperature variability in West Africa. Chapter 3 adopts a panel data analysis approach to examine food and nutrition security (FNS) and agricultural value-added nexus towards the realization of United Nations Sustainable Development Goals (UN SDGs) 2 in West Africa.

From a sustainable agricultural viewpoint, Chapter 4 analyzes the effect of infrastructural expansion on rural transformation, via increased investment agricultural research and development (R&D) in Nigeria.

Along similar discourse, Chapter 5 expatiates on the responsiveness of cassava and maize seed supply sustainability to public investment in R&D infrastructure in Nigeria.

While Chapter 6 presents a political economy understanding of the nutrition, health, climate change, deforestation and land access nexus in Africa, based on a few lessons from the United States, Chapter 7 adopts a gender lens in recommending policies for rural community development organizations towards alleviating poverty and malnutrition among women households and other vulnerable groups.

Chapter 8 assesses the short and long-run effect of agricultural production and farm management practices on Greenhouse Gas (GHG) Emissions in Cameroon. Chapter 9 uses data collected from structured questionnaires to conduct productivity analysis among smallholder rice farmers and the policy implications for nutrition security in Cameroon. Chapter 10 adopts the Ordinary Differential Equation (ODE) approach to examine how public expenditure and foreign direct investment could be leveraged for maximizing agricultural policy space in Cameroon.

The impact of climate change knowledge management cannot be overemphasized in enhancing nutrition and climate change adaptation capacities in Africa. In view of this, Chapter 11 epitomizes the role of modern knowledge management tools such as digital libraries in making African agriculture and policies much smarter. Finally, Chapter 12 concludes on the workable policy recommendations for fostering nutrition security and adapting to the changing climate through sustainable agriculture in a post-COVID-19 African ecosystem.

It is our expectation that readers and target audience will enjoy the nontechnical language which is adopted in discussing Africa's nutrition and sustainable agriculture prospects and challenges presented in this book and articulated by African practitioners and academics. It is written in a style that should interest anyone interested in Africa's nutrition and regional development. The references that support every chapter will expand readers' horizons of understanding and applying workable policy instruments and lessons for fostering Africa's nutritional outcomes.

References

Abrams, L., & Smedley, D. (2020). *Virtual Jobs: African Smallholder Farmers and Food Imports Report*. Stockholm: SIWI.

Africa Growth Initiative (AGI). (2017). *Ending Rural Hunger: The Cases of Ethiopia, Ghana, Nigeria, Senegal, Uganda and Tanzania*. The Brookings Institute Global Development Project on 'Ending Rural Hunger'. Retrieved from: www.endingruralhunger.org.

Allendorf, K. (2007). Do Women's Land Rights Promote Empowerment and Child Health in Nepal? *World Development, 35*(11), 1975–1988.

BMGF. (2012). *Optimising Nutrition Outcomes from Investments in Agriculture*. Seattle, WA: BMGF.

Child Health. (2020). WHO Regional Office for Africa 2020. *Child Health*. Accessed on August 2, 2020.

Covic, N., & Hendriks, S. I. (Eds). (2016). *Achieving a Nutrition Revolution for Africa: The Road to Healthier Diets and Optimal Nutrition* (ReSAKSS Annual Trends and Outlook Report). Washington, DC: International Food Policy Research Institute (IFPRI).

Dumas, S. E., Kassa, L., Young, S. L., & Travis, A. J. (2018). Examining the Association Between Livestock Ownership Typologies and Child Nutrition in the Luangwa Valley, Zambia. *PLOS One, 13*(2), e0191339. https://doi.org/10.1371/journal.pone.0191339.

FAO. (2010). *Africa's Changing Landscape: Securing Land Access for the Rural Poor*. Accra, Ghana: FAO Regional Office for Africa.

FAO. (2012). *Making Agriculture Work for Nutrition: Synthesis of Guiding Principles*. Rome: Italy.

FAO and WHO. (2013). *Impact Pathways from Agricultural Research to Improved Nutrition and Health: Literature Analysis and Research Priorities*. Rome: FAO, and WHO.

FAO, IFAD, UNICEF, WFP and WHO. (2017). *The State of Food Security and Nutrition in the World, 2017: Building Resilience for Peace and Food Security*. Rome, Italy.

Galiani, S., & Schargrodsky, E. (2004). Effects of Land Titling on Child Health. *Economics & Human Biology, 2*(3), 353–372.

Herforth, A., Jones, A., & Pinstrup-Andersen, P. (2012). *Prioritizing Nutrition in Agriculture and Rural Development: Guiding Principles for Operational Investments* (Health, Nutrition and Population Family [HNP] Discussion Paper). Washington, DC: World Bank.

Jones, M., Tambi, E., & Odularu, G. (2010, July 21). *Optimising Policy Space in the Context of Increasing International Support for CAADP.* South African Institute of International Affairs (SAIIA) Emerging Powers and Global Challenges Programme Policy Briefing. Retrieved from: https://saiia.org.za/

research/optimising-policy-space-in-the-context-of-increasing-international-support-for-caadp/.

Menon, N., van der Meulen Rodgers, Y., & Nguyen, H. (2014). Women's Land Rights and Children's Human Capital in Vietnam. *World Development, 54,* 18–31. https://doi.org/10.1016/j.worlddev.2013.07.005.

Owusu, J. S., Colecraft, E. K., Aryeetey, R., Vaccaro, J. A., & Huffman, F. G. (2016). Nutrition Intakes and Nutritional Status of School Age Children in Ghana. *Journal of Food Research.* Canadian Center of Science and Education. Retrieved from: https://www.researchgate.net/publication/313411333_Nutrition_Intakes_and_Nutritional_Status_of_School_Age_Children_in_Ghana. Accessed October 14, 2018 and October 5, 2019.

Sahn, D. E., & Younger, S. D. (2017). The Incidence of Child Health Improvements. *Review of Development Economics, 21*(2), 304–320. https://doi.org/10.1111/rode.12262.

Vogl, T. S. (2007). Urban Land Rights and Child Nutritional Status in Peru, 2004. *Economics & Human Biology, 5*(2), 302–321. https://doi.org/10.1016/j.ehb.2007.01.001.

World Bank. (2020, May 1). *The Impact of COVID-19 on Global Poverty: Why Sub-Saharan Africa Might Be the Region Hardest Hit*. https://blogs.worldbank.org/opendata/impact-covid–19-coronavirus-global-povery-why-sub-saharan-africa-might-be-region-hardest.

CHAPTER 2

Crop and Livestock Production Responses to Rainfall and Temperature Variation in West Africa

Ukpe Udeme Henrietta, Djomo Choumbou Raoul Fani, Ngo Valery Ngo, Oben Njock Emmanuel, and Gbadebo Odularu

U. U. Henrietta
Department of Agricultural Economics and Extension, Federal University Wukari, Wukari, Nigeria

D. C. R. Fani (✉)
Faculty of Agriculture and Veterinary Medicine, Department of Agricultural Economics and Agribusiness, University of Buea, Buea, Cameroon

N. V. Ngo
Section for Social Medicine and Epidemiology, Department of Global Health, The Sahlgrenska Academy,
University of Gothenburg, Gothenburg, Sweden

O. N. Emmanuel
Department of Agricultural Economics and Agribusiness,
University of Buea, Buea, Cameroon

G. Odularu
Department of Economics and Finance, Bay Atlantic University, Washington, DC, USA

G. Odularu (ed.), *Nutrition, Sustainable Agriculture and Climate Change in Africa*,
https://doi.org/10.1007/978-3-030-47875-9_2

Introduction

The agricultural sector has a multiplier effect on any nation's socio-economic and industrial fabric because of the multifunctional nature of the sector (Ogen 2007; Ayinde et al. 2011). It has the potential to be the industrial and economic springboard from which the country's development can take off (Stewart 2000; Ayinde et al. 2011). This sector remains the main source of livelihood for most rural communities in developing countries in general (Ayinde et al. 2011). In West Africa, agriculture is vital to livelihoods. It is the main source of employment for the 290 million people who live in the region, employing 60% of the workforce, and accounts for 35% of the region's gross domestic product (GDP) (Jalloh et al. 2013). This agricultural potential has made an investment in agriculture the backbone of overall growth and development for a majority of the countries in the region, and the key for poverty reduction and food security (Africa Agriculture Status Report [AGRA] 2014). This crucial economic activity is endangered by climate change (Jalloh et al. 2013).

Since agriculture in the region is dependent on rainfall, its farmers are particularly vulnerable to temperature and precipitation changes (Jalloh et al. 2013). Projections show that crop and fodder growing periods in western and southern Africa may shorten by an average of 20% by 2050, causing a 40% decline in cereal yields and a reduction in cereal biomass for livestock (Thornton et al. 2007, 2009a, b; FAO 2010; Lobell et al. 2011; Williams et al. 2015). Western, central and southern Africa may experience a decline in mean annual rainfall of 4, 5 and 5%, respectively (Hoerling et al. 2006; IPCC 2007, 2014; Williams et al. 2015). The threat that climate changes pose to agricultural production does not only cover the area of crop husbandry but also includes livestock and in fact the total agricultural sector. African farmers also depend on livestock for income, food and animal products (Nin et al. 2007; Ayinde et al. 2011). Climate can affect livestock both directly and indirectly (Adams et al. 1999; Manning and Nobrew 2001; Ayinde et al. 2011). Direct effects of climate variables such as air, temperature, humidity, wind speed and other climate factors influence animal performance such as growth, milk production, wool production and reproduction. Climate can also affect the quantity and quality of feedstuffs such as pasture, forage and grain and also the severity and distribution of livestock diseases and parasite (Niggol and Mendelsohn 2008; Ayinde et al. 2011). Hence the totality of the agricultural sector is considered by examining agricultural productivity (Ayinde et al. 2011).

This study adds valuable information for agricultural programmes and policy designs that can reduce risks of negative rainfall and temperature impact in West Africa's agricultural sector. It also enables to understand the impact of risk and uncertainty of rainfall and temperature predicting and forecasting crop and livestock subsector output in West Africa. Finally, identifying a region's comparative advantage in crop and livestock production due to climate change would help policymakers and the private sector in forward planning and adapting to changes in West Africa.

While there are several studies that investigate the relationship between climate change and agricultural production (Ahmed et al. 2012; Muller and Robertson 2014; Nakaegawa et al. 2012; Roudier et al. 2011; Asafu-Adjaye 2014), little or no attention has been made to the best of my knowledge to assess the simultaneous response of livestock and crop production to rainfall and temperature in West Africa. This study intends to fill the knowledge gap by analyzing crop and livestock production responses to rainfall and temperature variation in West Africa using Monte Carlo Simulation.

Methodology

The Study Area: This study was carried out in West Africa which is made of 16 countries namely: Ghana, Mali, Senegal, Burkina Faso, Benin, Niger, Sierra Leone, Togo, Liberia, Guinea, Gambia, Côte d'Ivoire, Nigeria, Cape-Verde, Guinea Bissau and Mauritania. West Africa's population has been growing fast and this trend is projected to continue until the middle of the century. Over the last thirty years, West Africa's population more than doubled, growing by 2.7% annually (UNDESA 2011; African Development Bank [AFDB] and the Food and Agriculture Organization of the United Nations [FAO] 2015). Agricultural production in the region is composed of many production systems and animal production but based mainly on very small-scale family-owned farms (of less than 10 hectares) (Blein et al. 2008).

Method of Data Collection: Due to the unavailability of data, annual time series covering a period of 50 years (1967–2016) were obtained to carry out the study. Specifically, data for crop and livestock subsector production; rainfall and temperature were obtained from the World Bank Development database indicators for the West African countries.

Techniques of Data Analysis: Ordinary least square was used to analyze the effect of rainfall and temperature on crop and livestock production. Monte Carlo Simulation was used to analyze effect of changes (involving three (3) scenarios at 25%) in rainfall and temperature on crop and livestock production.

Model Specification
Ordinary Least Square

$$Y_{it} = \beta_0 + \beta_{1it} X_{1it} + \beta_{2it} X_{2it} + \varepsilon_{it} \quad (2.1)$$

where

Y_{it} is crop or livestock production index (2004–2006) = 100 of ith country at time t (Tons)

X_{1it} is rainfall of ith country at time t (mm)

X_{2it} is temperature of ith country at time t (°C)

ε_{it} is error term.

Monte Carlo Simulation

$$E(f(X_i)) = \theta'_N = \frac{1}{N} \sum_{i=1}^{N} f(X_{it})$$

where X is a vector of rainfall and temperature

θ is the dependent variable (Y^*_{it}).

Crop and livestock subsectors production were simulated from the stochastic model,

$$Y^*_{it} = \alpha_{0i} + \alpha_1 * \left(X_{1it} + \vartheta_{1,it}\right) + \alpha_2 * \left(X_{2it} + \vartheta_{2,it}\right) + \zeta_{it} \quad (2.2)$$

where

Y^*_{it} is crop or livestock production index (2004–2006) = 100 of ith country at time t (Tons)

X_{1it} is rainfall of ith country at time t (mm)

X_{2it} is temperature of ith country at time t (°C)

$\vartheta_{1,\mathrm{it}}$ and $\vartheta_{2\mathrm{it}}$ = uncertainties in the measurement of X_{1it} and X_{2it}

ζ_{it} = exogenous white noise disturbance on the model.

Given the stochastic nature of this model, the behaviour of crop and livestock production under various scenarios was investigated. The simulation scenarios consist of increase in rainfall and decrease in temperature;

decrease in rainfall and increase in temperature; and increases rainfall and temperature by 25% each.

Results and Discussion

The result (Table 2.1) shows that 41.25 and 44.67% of the variation in crop and livestock subsector production is explained by rainfall and temperature, respectively. Further, the coefficient of temperature is positive and significant at 1% level of probability. This implies the increase in temperature increases crop production by the value of its estimated coefficient. This result agrees with some researchers who expect short-run gains in crop productivity with increases in temperature (Parry et al. 2004; Schlenker and Roberts 2009; Lambert 2014). This result is contrary to findings of Schlenker and Roberts' (2009) who found that temperature nonlinearities have major impacts on crop productivity such as days over 30 °C. However, under certain conditions the temperature can increase crop production as reported by Alocilja and Ritchie (1991), Baker et al. (1995) cited in Luo (2011), leaf photosynthesis rate of maize has a high Topt of 33–38 °C; Leaf-appearance rate increases with temperature from a Tbase of 8 °C, until reaching 36–40 °C, the thermal threshold of survival.

Table 2.1 Effect of rainfall and temperature on crop and livestock production in West Africa

Crop subsector production			*Livestock subsector production*		
Variables	*Coefficient*	t-*statistic*	*Variables*	*Coefficient*	t-*statistic*
Rainfall	0.002	1.504	Rainfall	0.010***	6.110
Temperature	4.368***	4.348	Temperature	5.448***	6.171
Constant	−46.231	−1.675	Constant	−84.625	−3.488
R-squared	0.4125		R-squared	0.4467	
Adjusted R-squared	0.4024		Adjusted R-squared	4365	
F-statistic	25.481		F-statistic	29.117	
Akaike info criterion	10.094		Akaike info criterion	9.836	
Durbin–Watson stat	0.257		Durbin–Watson stat	0.175	

Note N.B *** is significant at 1% probability level
Source Author's creation

The coefficient of rainfall is positive but not significant. Therefore, it has no significant effect on crop production.

As for livestock production, the coefficients for rainfall and temperature are positive and significant at 1% level of probability. This result implies that a unit increase in temperature and rainfall will increase livestock production. The increase in rainfall provides pasture which may be more productive if located in cooler and wetter climates and the land becomes more profitable for cattle and crops under these conditions. Grasslands will turn into forests, and hot, moist conditions will probably influence animal health (Gale et al. 2009; Semenza and Menne 2009; Rust and Rust 2013). However, there is a limit to the way in which dry landscapes can remain suitable for livestock. For an increase in temperature, farmers adapt to hot and dry climates by shifting to livestock. For small farmers, livestock provide some protection against the effects of warming, as crops become less desirable (Seo and Mendelssohn 2006; Rust and Rust 2013). These results are contrary to the findings of Abdela and Jilo (2016) who explained that global warming likely affects animal health by influencing the host–pathogen environment system both directly and indirectly (Table 2.2, 2.3 and Figs. 2.1, 2.2, 2.3).

Results show that increases (**scenario 3**) in temperature and rainfall provide the highest level of crop production index compare to scenarios 1 and 2 against the baseline. Some studies have shown that the impact of global warming in the mountainous area could have a positive impact for some vegetables and crops, such as tomato, cauliflower, wheat, maize and rice (Dahal 2005; Mishra et al. 2014; Poudel and Shaw 2016).

Table 2.2 Summary descriptive statistics of for average values of variables used in the model in West Africa

	Crop production index	*Livestock production index*	*Rainfall*	*Temperature*
Mean	73.79	72.39	1066.25	26.75
Median	67	70	1094.5	26.70
Maximum	236	214	2526	29.20
Minimum	19	14	92	21.95
Std. Dev.	37.97	34.17	707.73	1.38

Source Author's creation

Table 2.3 Descriptive statistics for simulated crop production index

	Baseline	*Scenario 1*	*Scenario 2*	*Scenario 3*
Mean	73.792	45.36	102.22	103.79
Median	73.96	45.73	102.69	104.01
Maximum	83.35	51.97	114.73	115.74
Minimum	50.32	26.52	74.12	74.46
Std. Dev.	5.789	4.52	7.25	7.23

Source Author's creation

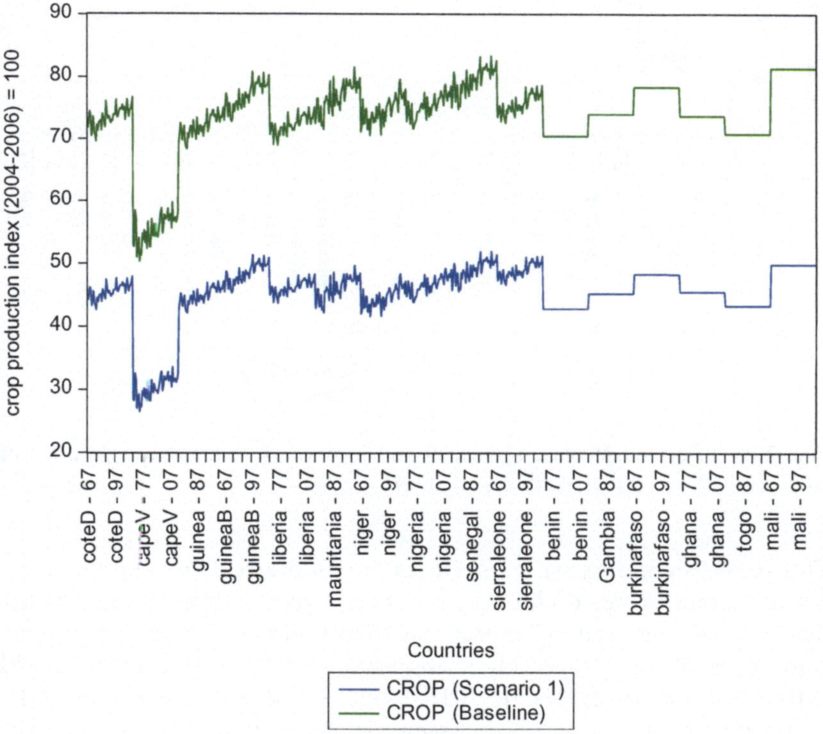

Fig. 2.1 Effect of increase in rainfall and decrease in temperature by 25% on crop production (*Source* Author's creation)

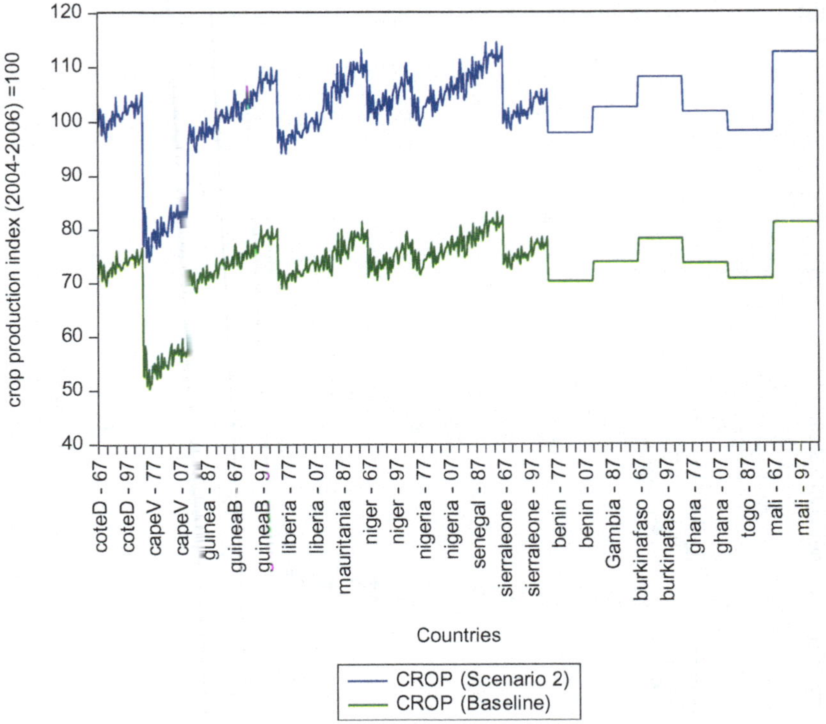

Fig. 2.2 Effect of decrease in rainfall and increase in temperature by 25% on crop production (*Source* Author's creation)

This result is contrary with a priori expectation given that extreme rainfall and temperature conditions are characterized by droughts and floods that can have devastating impacts on rural households engaged in agricultural production, especially in low-income regions around the world (Meza-Pale and Yunez-Naude 2015) (Figs. 2.4, 2.5, 2.6, and Table 2.4).

Results show that increases **(scenario 3)** in temperature and rainfall provide the highest level of livestock production index compare to scenarios 1 and 2 against the baseline. This result is contrary with a priori expectation given that excessive rainfall and temperature area associated with pest and disease attack which will thereby affect animal health and reduce livestock production.

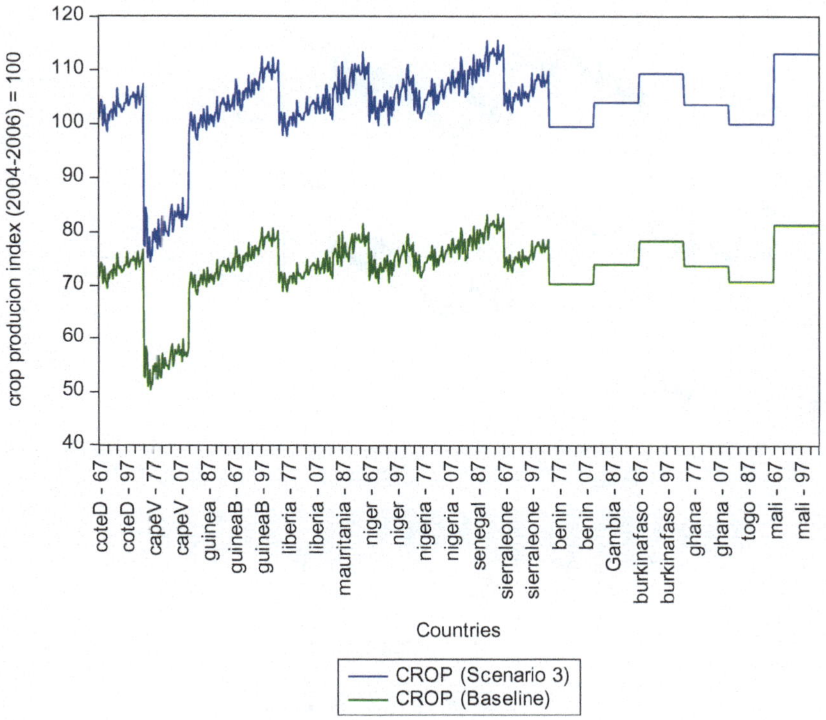

Fig. 2.3 Effect of increases in rainfall and temperature by 25% on crop production (*Source* Author's creation)

Conclusion

For the past decades, the international community raised alarming concerns of the probable negative impact of climatic variation on agricultural production. Despite policies set up there is a need to assess the extent to which climatic variation affect agricultural subsector production. This study assesses crop and livestock production responses to rainfall and temperature variation in West Africa for a period of 50 (1967–2016) years. It was found that 25% increases in rainfall and temperature provides the highest level of crop and livestock production in West Africa.

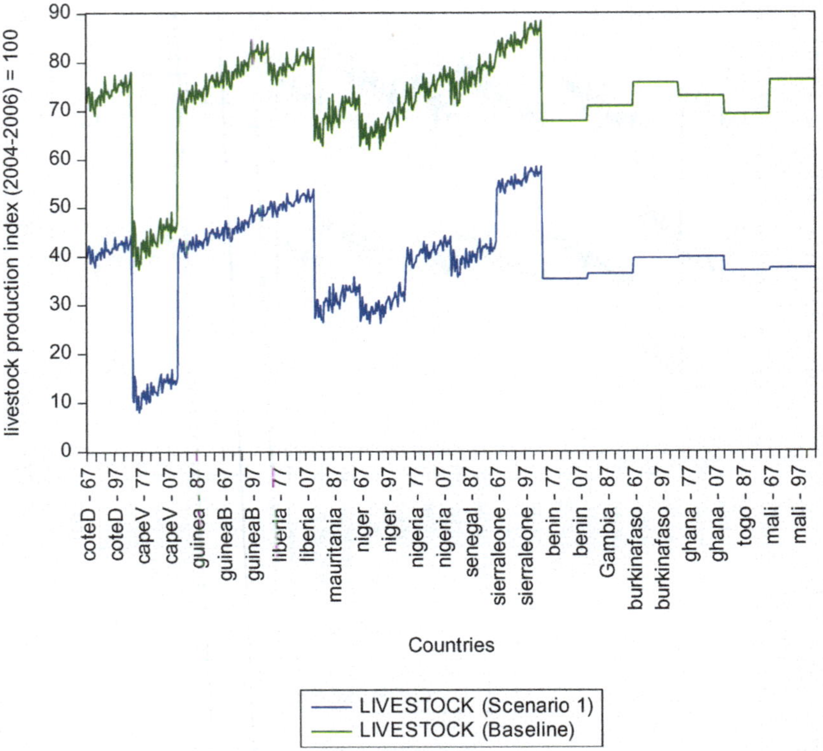

Fig. 2.4 Effect of increase in rainfall and decrease in temperature by 25% on livestock production (*Source* Author's creation)

Policy Recommendations

i. Strategies such as introduction of better floods warning systems, water storage areas and protection of wetlands should be implemented in West Africa given that increases in rainfall and temperature may likely cause floods and drought in the region if appropriate measures are implemented.

ii. Reforestation policy through increment in budgetary allocation to the ministry of forestry should be implemented in the dry land

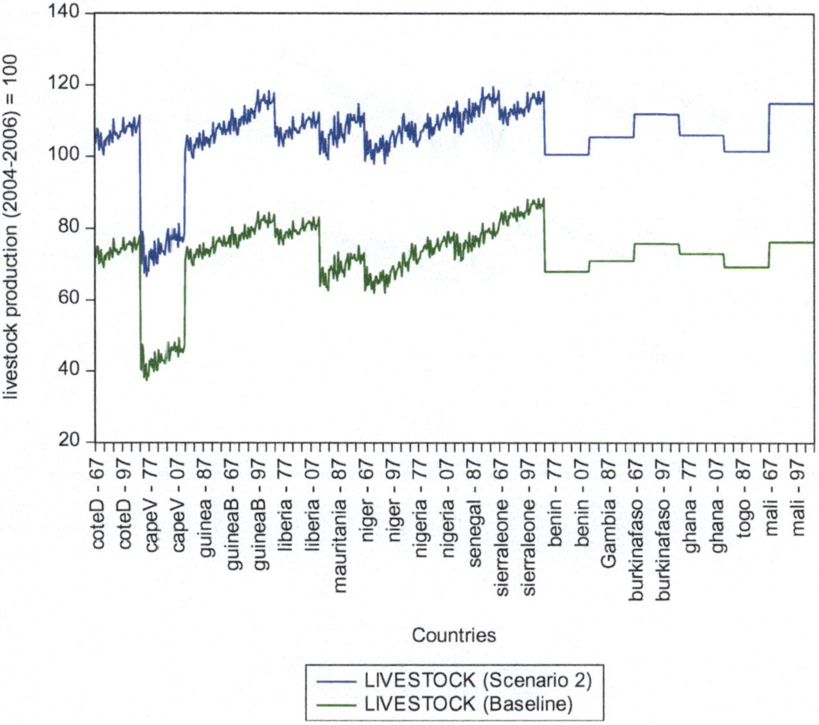

Fig. 2.5 Effect of decrease in rainfall and increase in temperature by 25% on livestock production (*Source* Author's creation)

zone of West Africa due to the fact that it is paramount to regulate constant increase of temperature given that there is a thermal threshold (38 °C–40 °C)for agricultural production.

iii. Regional laws prohibiting deforestation should be established in order to protect the existing ecosystem which will sustain the current level of climatic variation for agricultural production.

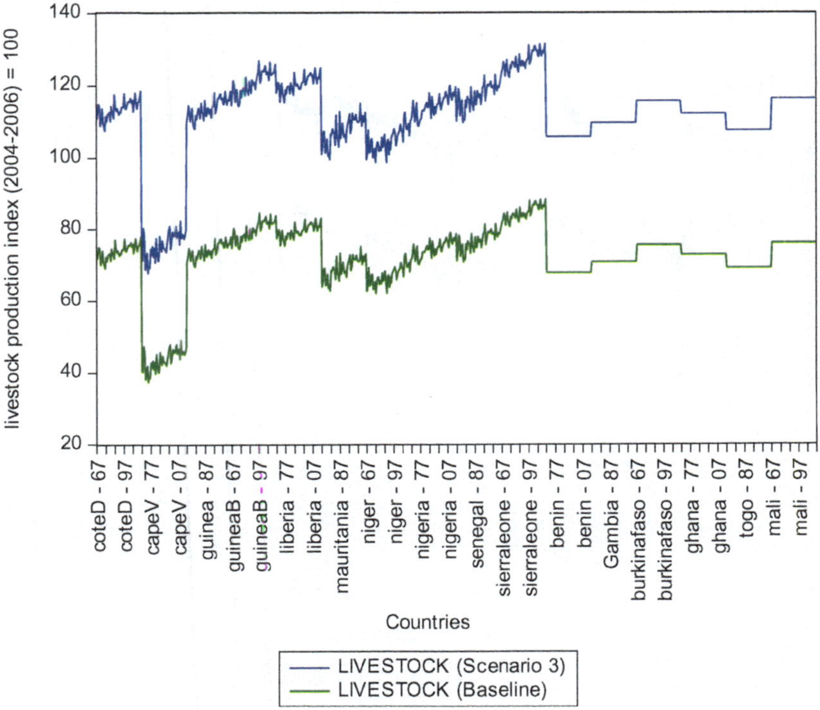

Fig. 2.6 Effect of increases in rainfall and temperature by 25% on livestock production (*Source* Author's creation)

Table 2.4 Descriptive statistics for simulated livestock production index

	Baseline	*Scenario 1*	*Scenario 2*	*Scenario 3*
Mean	72.39	38.77	106.02	111.65
Median	73.39	39.65	106.73	112.90
Maximum	88.51	58.56	119.67	131.80
Minimum	37.37	8.07	66.66	67.87
Std. Dev.	8.91	9.38	9.44	11.14

Source Author's creation

References

Abdela, N., & Jilo, K. (2016). Impact of Climate Change on Livestock Health: A Review. *Global Veterinaria, 16* (5), 419–424. https://doi.org/10.5829/idosi.gv.2016.16.05.10370.

Adams, R. M., McCarl, B. A., Segerson, K., Rosenzweig, C., Bryant, K. J., Dixon, B. L., et al. (1999). The Economic Effects of Climate Change on US Agriculture. *The Impact of Climate Change on the United States Economy*, 18–54.

Africa Agriculture Status Report (AGRA). (2014). *Climate change and Smallholder Agriculture in Sub-saharan Africa*. Nairobi, Kenya. Alliance for a Green Revolution in Africa. Retrieved from https://ccafs.cgiar.org/publications/africa-agriculture-status-report-2014-climate-change-and-smallholder-agriculturesub#.XxxJKJ5KjIU.

African Development Bank (AFDB) and the Food and Agriculture Organization of the United Nations (FAO). (2015). *Agricultural Growth in West Africa: Market and Policy Drivers*. Rome.

Ahmed, S., Noah, S. D., Thomas, W. H., & William, J. M. (2012). *Agriculture and Trade Opportunities for Tanzania: Past Volatility and Future Climate Change* (Policy Research Working Paper 6132). The World Bank Development Research Group Agriculture and Rural Development Team. Washington, DC: World Bank.

Alocilja, E. C., & Ritchie, J. T. (1991). A Model for the Phenology of Rice. Chapter 15. In T. Hodges (Ed.), *Predicting Crop Phenology* (pp. 181–189). Boca Raton: CRC.

Asafu-Adjaye, J. (2014). The Economic Impacts of Climate Change on Agriculture in Africa. *Journal of African Economies, 23*(AERC Supplement 2), ii17–ii49. https://doi.org/10.1093/jae/eju011.

Ayinde, O. E., Muchie, M., & Olatunji, G. B. (2011). Effect of Climate Change on Agricultural Productivity in Nigeria: A Co-integration Model Approach. *Journal of Human Ecology, 35*(3), 189–194.

Baker, J. T., Boote, K. J., & Allen Jr., L. H. (1995). Potential Climate Change Effects on Rice: Carbon Dioxide Andtemperature. In C. Rosenzweig, J. W. Jones, & L. H. Jr Allen (Eds.), *Climate Change and Agriculture: Analysis of Potential International Impacts* (pp. 31–47). ASA Special Pub. No. 59. Madison, WI: American Society of Agronomy.

Blein, R., Soulé, B. G., Dupaigre, B. F., & Yerima, B. (2008). *Agricultural Potential of West Africa (ECOWAS)*. Report Prepared for the FARM Foundation in Collaboration with IRAM, ISSALA, and LARES. Available at: http://www.fondation-farm.org/IMG/pdf/etudepotentialites_rapport.pdf.

Dahal, N. (2005). *Perceptions of Climate Change in the Himalaya; Tiempo Climate Change Bulletin*. Stockholm, Sweden.

FAO (Food and Agriculture Organization of the United Nations). (2010, May 3–7). *Climate Change Implications for Food Security and Natural Resources Management in Africa*. Background Paper Prepared for the Twenty-Sixth Regional Conference for Africa (ARC/10/8). Luanda, Angola.

Gale, P., Brouwer, A., Ramnial, V., Kelly, L., Kosmider, R., Fooks, A. R., et al. (2010). Assessing the Impact of Climate Change on Vector-Borne Viruses in the EU Through the Elicitation of Expert Opinion. *Epidemiology & Infection*, 1–12.

Hoerling, M., Hurrel, J., Eischeid, J., & Phillips, A. (2006). Detection and Attribution of Twentieth-Century Northern and Southern African Rainfall Change. *Journal of Climate, 19*, 3989–4008.

Intergovernmental Panel on Climate Change. (2007). Summary for Policymakers. In M. L. Parry et al. (Eds.), *Climate Change 2007: Impacts, Adaptation and Vulnerability—Contribution of Working Group II to the Fourth Assessment Report of the Intergovernmental Panel on Climate Change*. Cambridge and New York: Cambridge University Press.

Intergovernmental Panel on Climate Change. (2014). *Climate Change 2014: Impacts, Adaptation and Vulnerability. IPCCWGIIAR5 Technical Summary*. Available at: http://ipccwg2.gov/AR5/images/uploads/WGIIAR5-TS_FGDall.pdf. Accessed on August 19, 2014.

Jalloh, A., Nelson, G. C., Thomas, T. S., Zougmoré, R., & Roy-Macauley, H. (2013). *West African Agriculture and Climate Change: A Comprehensive Analysis* (IFPRI Issue Brief, 75).

Lambert, D. K. (2014). Historical impacts of Precipitation and Temperature on Farm Production in Kansas. *Journal of Agricultural and Applied Economics, 46*(4), 439–456.

Lobell, D. B., Bänziger, M., Magorokosho, C., & Vivek, B. (2011). Nonlinear Heat Effects on African Maize as Evidenced by Historical Yield Trials. *Nature Climate Change, 1*, 42–45.

Luo, Q. (2011). Temperature Thresholds and Crop Production: A Review. *Climatic Change, 109*, 583–598. https://doi.org/10.1007/s10584-011-0028-6.

Manning, M., & Nobrew, C. (2001). Technical Summary Impact, Adaption and Vulnerability: A Report of Working Group II of the Intergovernmental Panel on Climate Change. In J. McCarthy, O. F. Canziani, N. A. Leavy, J. D. Dekken, & C. White (Eds.), *Climate Change 2001: Impact, Adaption and Vulnerability* (pp. 44–65). Cambridge: Cambridge University Press.

Mishra, B., Babel, M. S., & Tripathi, N. K. (2014). Analysis of Climatic Variability and Snow Cover in the Kaligandaki River Basin, Himalaya, Nepal. *Theoretical and Applied Climatology, 116*, 681–694.

Meza-Pale, P., & Yunez-Naude, A. (2015, August 8–14). *The Effect of Rainfall Variation on Agricultural Households: Evidence from Mexico.* 29th International Conference of Agricultural Economists.

Muller, C., & Robertson, R. D. (2014). Projecting Future Crop Productivity for Global Economic Modeling. *Agricultural Economics, 45*(1), 37–50.

Nakaegawa, T., Wachana, C., & KAKUSHIN Team-3 Modeling Group. (2012). First Impact Assessment of Hydrological Cycle in the Tana River Basin, Kenya, Under a Changing Climate in the Late 21st Century. *Hydrological Research Letters, 6*, 29–34.

Niggol, S., Mendelsohn, R. (2008). Animal Husbandry in Africa: Climate Impacts and Adaptations. *AfJARE,* 2(1), 66.

Nin, A., Ehui, S., & Benin, S. (2007). Livestock Productivity in Developing Countries: An Assessment. In R. Evenson & P. Pingali (Eds.), *Handbook of Agricultural Economics* (Vol. 3, pp. 2467–2532). North Holland: Oxford Press.

Ogen, O. (2007). The Agricultural Sector and Nigeria's Development: Comparative Perspectives from the Brazilian Agro-Industry Economy 1960–1995. *Nebula, 4*(10), 184–194.

Parry, M. L., Rosenzweig, C., Iglesias, A., Livermore, M., & Fisher, G. (2004). Effects of Climate Change on Global Food Production Under SRES Emissions and Socio-Economic Scenarios. *Global Environmental Change, 14*(1), 53–67.

Poudel, S., & Shaw, R. (2016). The Relationships Between Climate Variability and Crop Yield in a Mountainous Environment: A Case Study in Lamjung District, Nepal. *Climate, 4*(1), 13.

Roudier, P., Sultan, B., Quirion, P., & Berg, A. (2011). The Impact of Future Climate Change on West African Crop Yields: What Does the Recent Literature Say? *Global Environmental Change, 21*(3), 1073–1083.

Rust, J. M., & Rust, T. (2013). Climate Change and Livestock Production: A Review with Emphasis on Africa. *South African Journal of Animal Science, 43*(3), 255–267.

Seo, S. N., & Mendelsohn, R. (2006). *Climate Change Impacts on Animal Husbandry in Africa: A Ricardian Analysis* (CEEPA Discussion Paper No. 9). Pretoria, South Africa: Centre for Environmental Economics and Policy in Africa, University of Pretoria.

Semenza, J. C., & Menne, B. (2009). Climate Change and Infectious Diseases in Europe. *Lancet ID, 9*, 365–375.

Stewart, R. (2000). Welcome Address. In *Proceedings of the 7th World Sugar Conference*. Durbar.

Schlenker, W., & Roberts, M. J. (2009). Nonlinear Temperature Effects Indicate Severe Damages to U.S. Crop Yields under Climate Change. *Proceedings of the National Academy of Sciences of the United States of America, 106*(37), 15594–15598.

Thornton, P., Herrero, M., Freeman, A., Mwai, O., Rege, E., Jones, P., et al. (2007). *SATeJournal, ejournal.icrisat.org, 4*(1), 1–23. Available at: http://www.icrisat.org/journal/SpecialProject/sp7.pdf. Accessed on July 14, 2014.

Thornton, P. K., Jones, P. G., Alagarswamy, G., & Andresen, J. (2009a). Spatial Variation of Crop Yield Response to Climate Change in East Africa. *Global Environmental Change, 19,* 54–65.

Thornton, P. K., van de Steeg, J., Notenbaert, A., & Herrero, M. (2009b). The Impacts of Climate Change on Livestock and Livestock Systems in Developing Countries: A Review of What We Know and What We Need to Know. *Agricultural Systems, 101,* 113–127.

UNDESA. (2011). *World Population Prospects, 2011 Revision.* United Nations Department of Economic and Social Affairs (UNDESA).

Williams, T. O., Mul, M., Cofie, O., Kinyangi, J., Zougmore, R., Wamukoya, G., et al. (2015). *Climate Smart Agriculture in the African Context*. Feeding Africa, an Action Plan for Agricultural Transformation in Africa, Abdou Diouf International Conference Center, pp. 1–22.

CHAPTER 3

Agricultural Value Added, Food and Nutrition Security in West Africa: Realizing the SDG 2

Romanus Osabohien, Oluwatoyin Matthew, Folasade Adegboye, and Gbadebo Odularu

Introduction

Food security simply means a situation where all people, at all times, have physical, social and economic access to sufficient, safe and nutritious food that meets their dietary needs and food preferences for an active and healthy life (Food and Agriculture Organisation [FAO] 2017). Food security goes beyond availability. It includes ability to possess monetary and non-monetary resources by the population to gain access to adequate

R. Osabohien (✉) · O. Matthew
Department of Economics and Development Studies, Covenant University, Ota, Nigeria
e-mail: romanus.osabohien@covenantuniversity.edu.ng

F. Adegboye
Department of Banking and Finance, Covenant University, Ota, Nigeria

G. Odularu
Department of Economics and Finance, Bay Atlantic University, Washington, DC, USA

G. Odularu (ed.), *Nutrition, Sustainable Agriculture and Climate Change in Africa*,
https://doi.org/10.1007/978-3-030-47875-9_3

quantities and qualities of food (Osabohien et al. 2020; Schmidhuber and Tubiello 2007; Osabohien et al. 2018a). One of the major ways to ensure food security is to engage in agriculture, this will help sustain increase in agricultural produce that the teeming population will get food from (Osabohien et al. 2020).

Agriculture also serves as the main employer of labour as well as a source of raw materials to the few available industries in West Africa and some other foreign countries, while agricultural value added simply refers to the increasing the economic value of agricultural commodities through a production processes; for example; organic produce, or through regionally branded products that increase consumer appeal and willingness to pay a premium over similar but undifferentiated products. What people will expect from countries in this sub-region is food security. Although, World Food Summit (WFS) has commended the progress noted in the area of achieving the Millennium Development Goals (MDGs) in West Africa compared to other sub-Saharan African countries, having reduced the number of undernourished people by almost 13 million between 1990–1992 and 2014–2016. However, improvement in this area is still needed (Benson 2008). It has been noted that, on average, out of 280 million people living in West Africa, 17% are still food insecure, about 30% live below the poverty line, 33% of children under five years of age are stunted, 28.3% are underweight and 10% are wasted (Tol 2002a, b; Matthew et al. 2018b).

Although agricultural growth is not the only stimulating factor of the economy in West Africa, but it is the most important contributor to manufacturing and service activity. It has also been noted that, each unit increase in agricultural activity leads to approximately 1.5 units of economic growth (Lam et al. 2012; Tol 2002a, b; Swallow 2005; Osabohien et al. 2019). Some studies have also noted the positive relation between economic growth and food security (Di Falco et al. 2011; Nellemann and MacDevette 2009), it has been observed that economic growth reduces income poverty more than promoting food security (Pearce et al. 1996), some found negative relation in some regions of the world (Love and Zicchino 2006) and yet others find no relation between the two (IFPRI 2005).

Food security is one of the major recent threats confronting the world. Food security is interlinked with other current global challenges of economy, weather and climatic change. The best way of determining the sufficiency is when households, at every given time, are able to afford food; safe, sufficient and energy given food that meets their daily need of food consumption. This connotes enhancing households' entitlements to food (Atinmo and Adeniran 1999; Barrett and Palm 2016). The economic and environmental concerns in recent years have exacerbated global food security problems. A probable outcome of global warming suggests that a large part of the African continent will become drier and experience massive climatic fluctuations, which would have serious consequences for the region with over 70% of the population being dependent on agriculture (Sen and Drèze 1989; Osabohien et al. 2018b; Matthew et al. 2018a).

It has been observed from past studies that African youth prefer 'white collar' jobs to getting engaged in the agricultural sector. This assertion was buttressed in the study of Collinson et al. (2016), using descriptive study to examine youth migration, livelihood prospects and demographic dividend in rural northeast of South Africa. They found out that only 10% male youth were employed in the agricultural sector in 2000 and this reduced to 3% in 2012. Similarly, the percentage of female youths employed in the agricultural sector witnessed a reduction from 11% in 2000 to 6% in 2012. They observed that the remaining parts of the population in both years were employed in other sectors of the economy. The study recommended that for employment in agriculture to increase more youths should be engaged in it and this would help reduce unemployment and reduce poverty. It is in the light of the above that this study aimed to examine how agricultural value addiction will help achieve food security in ECOWS. This is germane because, SGD 2 is timed towards food security

Literature Review

The largest number of the people who are living below the poverty line are from two main regions: 'Southern Asia and sub-Saharan Africa' and it is observed that two in five children aged five and below in these regions have insufficient height for their age due to undernourishment (FAO 2017). According to the study by Diao et al. (2009), which examined the effect of poverty reduction and overall growth rate of other growth channels in six low-income African countries, poverty reduction industrial growth is less effective than agricultural growth because a significant percentage (about 70%) of the population lives in rural areas (Osabohien et al. 2019). The agricultural sector is beneficial because it allows the poor to have more job opportunities. Diao et al. (2009) also noted that while it is important for the industrial sector to boost the economy, it does not provide sufficient employment opportunities for the poor and the unqualified. Moreover, the study stated that there was little evidence to prove that African countries could initiate a successful economic transformation without undergoing an agricultural revolution across the country.

It is recognised that the food produced globally is sufficient in meeting the needs of the present world's population. Chen and Kates (1994) agreed with the above statement and argued that the issue of food security faced globally is not due to the scarcity of food, but it is people's entitlement to food that enhances their access to food which they lack. Chen and Kates (1994) believed that the idea of food entitlement posits the issue of insecurity of food and continuous malnutrition as the main determinants of low-income elasticity of those who are deprived of the necessary ability for both to manufacture food or the fiscal capability required to acquire food in a continuous way (Atinmo and Adeniran 1999). In the same vein, access to food is the main determinant of food security than the availability of food. They pointed out that the problem of food insecurity is transitory and not chronic (this means that it can be controlled as per the given time if food production base can be increased and enhancement of individual's access to produced food).

The Sustainable Development Goals (SDGs) which succeeded the Millennium Development Goals (MDGs) envisaged that by the year 2030 there would be enough food for all (food security, SDG Goal 2). Food insecurity and hunger are forerunners to nutritional, health, human and economic and sustainable development problems of any nation (Fasoyiro and Taiwo 2012; Matthew et al. 2019). How far these goes can be realised will be unfolded in the process of time just as the Millennium Development Goals (MDGs) were not adequately attained in Nigeria, the dawn of the end period of December 2015 (Osabohien et al. 2018a). For instance, in Africa, more than 75 million of its citizens have little or no access to food which is required to meet their daily energy needs (Bamisaye 1987; Obayelu 2015; Afolayan et al. 2019).

Furthermore, less emphasis is made in proffering solutions to the achievement of economic development through the tool of agriculture. Ogbalubi and Wokocha (2013) conducted an empirical investigation and found that agricultural sector has significant potential for the African economy transformation. The study further recognised that West Africa's most important public policies are tailored towards food security, supplying the manufacturing sector with agricultural raw materials needed to provide adequate employment and income. The study recommended providing farmers with credit, extension services, price stabilisation and prioritising agriculture to enhance its value. In the same vein, Gustavo and Kostas (2007) investigated the relationship between rurality and poverty as well as the role they play in rural development and poverty reduction.

Eliamoni et al. (2015) used a descriptive analysis to examine the role of agriculture in Tanzania's economic growth and poverty reduction from 1980 to 2014. The study shows that an increase in population (household size in rural areas) and poor public services in rural areas exacerbated the poverty condition and accelerate shifting from agriculture to non-agricultural activities especially the educated youth. The study recommended that more people should be encouraged to practice farming in the rural areas and soft loans should be provided to the farmers if the nation wants to continue pursuing a high level of achievement in the provision of arable land. In addition, there should be favourable climate which will help increase food production thereby ensuring the availability of supply of agricultural produce.

Olofin et al. (2015) using annual data from 1990 to 2014 examined the effect of income growth and government effectiveness on food security in West African Countries. The result of the Ordinary Least Square method of estimation used showed that there is a positive and significant relationship between income growth and food security while a positive relationship exists between government effectiveness and food security. The study recommends that government effectiveness and income growth are important in attaining food security in West African Countries. Fawole et al. (2015) using Nigeria as a case study examined the causes, effect and solutions to food insecurity in Africa. Using descriptive analysis (tables and graphs), the study found that the indicators of food security were rising in Nigeria during the study period thus posing a threat to food security issues in the country and Africa at large. The study identified the causes of food insecurity to include urbanisation, war and political instability, population growth, climate change among others. Provision of infrastructure and storage facilities, population control, reliable agricultural policy among others are the solutions provided to abolish food insecurity issues in the country and Africa at large. This study contributes to knowledge in this regard pointing out how the governments of West African countries can improve on agricultural value in order to ensure food security.

Methodology

The empirical model for this study is related closely to the empirical work of Osabohien et al. (2018a), where it was argued that agriculture credit leads to food security through the creation of employment opportunities and increase the level of the income of households who engage in agriculture. The insight of the fixed effect model is from the work of Osuma et al. (2018). Thus, the implicit form of the model is expressed in Eq. (3.1) as:

$$\text{FOODSEC}_{it} = f\left(\text{AGRICVAR}_{it}, \text{PSAV}_{it,}, \text{ACE}_{it}, \text{POP}_{it}\right) \quad (3.1)$$

Equation (3.1) is the implicit form of the model, the explicit (non-linear log) form of the model is expressed in Eq. (3.2) as:

$$FOODSEC_{it}^{k} = A.AGRCVAR_{it}^{\alpha_1 N}.PSAV_{it}^{\alpha_2}.ACE_{it}^{\alpha_3}.POP_{it}^{\alpha_4 j}.\mu_{it} \quad (3.2)$$

Equation (3.2) can be double log linearised as shown in Eq. (3.3)

$$\begin{aligned}\text{logFOODSEC}l_{it}^{k} = &\alpha_0 + \alpha_1\text{logAGRICVAR}_{it}^{N} + \alpha_2\text{logPSAV}_{it} \\ &+ \alpha_3\text{logACE}_{it} + \alpha_4\text{logPOP}_{it}^{j} + \mu \quad (3.3)\end{aligned}$$

where; FOODSEC represents food security, GRICVAR represents agricultural variables included in this study, PSAV is political stability and absence of violence, ACE represents access to electricity, and POP represents population, it represents entities (fifteen ECOWAS countries) and time (2000–2017), respectively log represent logarithm form, α_0 represent the constant term, $\alpha_1, \alpha_{2,}\alpha_{3,}\alpha_4$ represent the coefficient of the exogenous variables, μ presents the error term.

The sustainable Development Goals (SDGs) implemented by the United Nations to be achieved by 2030, has 17 goals and 169 targets; this study is in line with Goal 2: which is to ensure zero hunger/food security. Food security exists when all people at all times have physical, social and economic access to sufficient, safe and nutritious food to meet their dietary needs and food preferences for an active and healthy life (FAO 2018). Basically, there are four main components of food security, which include: availability, accessibility, utilisation and stability. This study used two main indicators of food security (Sustainable Development Goal 2) as shown in Eq. (3.3), $K = 2$: availability and accessibility. Food access is proxied by gross domestic per capital, purchasing power parity (PPP) (constant 1$ per person), while food availability is proxied by the average value of food production. It unarguable that agriculture is a baseline for the achievement of food security; therefore, in our model, $N = 3$ representing three agricultural variables included which are: agriculture employment, agriculture value added and agriculture production. $j = 3$; Fertility rate, total population and population growth rate. The summary of variables included in the model is presented in Table 3.1.

Results

The analysis was done using the fixed-effects regression model. To determine the suitability of the fixed-effects or the random effects model, the 'Hausman' test was conducted where the null hypothesis is that the preferred model is the fixed-effects. The major advantage of the fixed-effects model is that, the fixed-effects model controls for all time-invariant differences between the individuals, so the estimated coefficients of the fixed-effects models are not biased as a result of the omitted time-invariant characteristics (Osuma et al. 2018; Greene 2008). Another important assumption of the fixed effect model is that those time-invariant characteristics are unique to the individual and are not correlated with other individual characteristics (Greene 2008). Each entity is different therefore; the entities error term and the constant (which captures individual characteristics) are not correlated with the others, and this helps to obtain estimates that are BLUE-Best Linear, Unbiased Estimators (Ejemeyovwi et al. 2018).

This section presents the estimated outcomes from the fixed regression model as shown in Tables 3.2 and 3.3 for the two proxies of food security in this study.

Table 3.2 presents the result obtained from the first indicator, average value of food production as a proxy for food availability. The average of food production dimension of food availability component of food security expresses the food net production value available to the people. Variables included in the model are; as determinants of food production; agricultural production, agriculture employment, agriculture valued added, political stability and absence of violence, access to electricity, fertility rate, population and population growth. From the result, the variable is statistically significant in explaining the level of food production in West Africa.

Table 3.1 Summary of variables

Data	*Identifier*	*Source*	*Definition and measurement*	*Mean*	*Std*	*Min*	*Max*
Food Access	GDPPC	FAO	GDP per capita at 1$ per person	2208.4	1324.8	579.1	6074.8
Availability	AVFP	FAO	Average value of food production (constant 1$ per person)	153.3	58.7	60	285
Agriculture Production	AGRICP	WDI	Agriculture % of GDP	29.9	13.9	6.4	79.0
Agriculture employment	AGRICEMP	WDI	Employment in agriculture, total (% of total employment	55.6	16.1	27.1	85.7
Agriculture value added	AGRIVVA	WDI	Agriculture value added per person	1311.6	944.9	383.1	6057.9
Political Stability and Absence of Violence	PSAV	WDI	Institutions	−0.5	0.8	−2.4	1.22
Population	POP	WDI 2017	Population, total	1.7	3.7	435,079	1.7e
Population Growth Rate	POPG	WDI		2.6	0.6	1.0	5.3
Fertility Rate	FR			5.3	0.9	2.6	6.9
Access to Electricity	ACESS		Access to electricity % of total population	33.6	20.5	0.0	90.1

Note WDI is World Development Indicators; FAO is Food and agriculture Organization
Source Authors' Compilation, 2019

Table 3.2 Food availability result (proxy/dependent variable: Average value of food production)

Variable	*1*	*2*	*3*	*4*	*5*	*6*
Agriculture production	0.0167** (0.0034) [0.0000]	0.2317** (0.0914) [0.091]	–	–	–	0.0053* (0.0013) [0.000]
Agriculture employment	–	–	0.3983* (0.1490) [0.0000]	–	–	–
Agriculture value added	–	–	–	0.40,141* (0.1105) [0.001]	–	–
Political Stability and Absence of Violence	0.05,969** (0.0255) [0.0019]	0.0142** (0.0146) [0.0360]	0.5686* (1.7890) [0.002]	0.01,928* (0.0155) [0.0002]	0.01,593 (0.0151) [0.299)	–
Population	–	–	−0.0207* (1.7807) [0.0005]	–	−0.2852 (0.3110) [0.3640]	−0.4150* (0.1007) [0.0000]

(continued)

Table 3.2 (continued)

Variable	*1*	*2*	*3*	*4*	*5*	*6*
Access to Electricity	–	0.4249*	–	–	0.5705*	–
		(0.0899)			(0.1929)	
		[0.0000]			[0.0005]	
Fertility Rate	−0.6668	−0.05,867*	−0.13,816		−0.78,662	−0.2995
	(0.8034)	(0.2490)	(4.1984)		(0.2369)	(0.1918)
	[0.000]	[0.000]	[0.787)		[0.0020]	[0.1200]
Constant	12.37,971*	2.5686*	96.2318*	78.7674	6.0723	−1.2480
	(0.4516)	(0.6024)	(27.6634)	(9.5118)	(4.1476)	(1.8550]
	[0.0000]	[0.000]	[0.0001]	[0.000]	[0.1500]	[0.5020]
R.sq Overall	0.8944	0.5412	0.5932	0.5816	0.5067	0.5063
Prob > F	0.0000	0.0000	0.0000	0.0000	0.0000	0.0000
	F(14, 158) = 482.63	F(8, 48) = 175.77	F(8, 48) = 175.77	F(14, 158) = 482.63	F(8, 47) = 31.51	F(14, 173) = 185.92
Year Dummies	No	No	No	No	No	No
Country Dummies	No	No	No	No	No	No
Robust S.E	Yes	Yes	Yes	Yes	Yes	Yes

Note () and [] represents standard error *t*-statistic, respectively. * and ** means that coefficients are significant at 1% and 5%, respectively. Variables are in their log form

Source Authors' Computation, 2019

Table 3.3 Food access result (proxy/dependent variable: GDP Per capita [constant $1 per person])

Variable	*1*	*2*	*3*	*4*	*5*	*6*
Agriculture production	–	0.2904* (0.1426) [0.0760]	–	0.2590 (0.1637) [0.1510]	–	0.6309* (0.1010) [0.0000]
Agriculture employment	–	0.3843 (0.3102) [0.2500]	–	–	0.3417* (0.1001) [0.0040]	0.8369* (0.1683) [0.0001]
Agriculture value added	0.1755** (0.0622) [0.0230]	–	–	0.26,215* (0.0502) [0.0010]	0.4580* (0.0613) [0.0000]	0.7237* (0.0250) [0.000]
Political Stability and Absence of Violence	0.0297*** (0.0158) (0.0970)	0.0221 ** (0.0095) [0.048]	0.0301** (0.0133) (0.0540)	0.0386** (0.0124) [0.0150]	–	0.0124 (0.0067) [0.1050]
Population Growth	– 0.4418* (0.0540) [0.0000]	– 0.3386* (0.0709) [0.001]	–	–0.5151* (0.0667) [0.0000]	0.5390* (0.0658) [0.0000]	0.3796** (0.1163) [0.0110]
Access to Electricity	0.3630*** (0.1236) [0.0190]	0.3720** (0.1189) [0.0140]	–	–	–	–

(continued)

Table 3.3 (continued)

Variable	*1*	*2*	*3*	*4*	*5*	*6*
Fertility Rate	–	–	–0.1919*	–	–	–
			(0.1850)			
			[0.0000]			
Constant	5.6785*	7.6701*	11.1913*	–4.3555	–5.5352*	–4.4589**
	(0.4229)	(0.7056)	(1.1342)	(3.3432)	(1.6775)	(1.6223)
	[0.0000]	[0.000]	[0.0000]	[0.2290]	[0.0005]	[0.025]
R.sq Overall	0.8232	0.8198	0.7897	0.8472	0.7295	0.9195
Prob > F	0.0000	0.0000	0.0000	0.0000	0.0000	0.0000
	F(4,8) = 114.60	F(4,8) = 449.26	F(3,8) = 38.19	F(5,8) = 123.75	F(3,14) = 30.12	F(5,8) = 608.61
Year Dummies	No	No	No	No	No	No
Country Dummies	No	No	No	No	No	No
Robust S.E	Yes	Yes	Yes	Yes	Yes	Yes
'A priori' expectation	Yes	Yes	Yes	Yes	Yes	Yes

Note () and [] represents standard error *t*-statistic, respectively. * and ** means that coefficients are significant at 1 and 5%, respectively
Source Authors' Computation, 2019

Agricultural production, agriculture employment, valued added, political stability and absence of violence and access to electricity are positively related to the average value of food production; this implies that a 1% increase in these variables, all things being equal, will bring about a positive increase in food production. Agriculture production contributes 16.7, 23.17 and 0.05% increase to food security, employment increase food security by approximately 39%, valued added 40.1%, political stability and absence of violence 14.2, 56.9, 1.9, 1.5%, electricity access 42.5 and 57%.

From this result, this can be unarguably inferred that agriculture production, employment in the agriculture sector and agriculture value added per worker which is a measure of agricultural productivity and measures the total output of the agricultural sector should be enhanced through agriculture credit facilities (Osabohien et al. 2018b). Credit facilities to the agricultural sector will make agriculture more fashionable for the young people to be involved in, thereby enhance the productive capacity of the sector and in the long-run increased food security.

Therefore, achieving Sustainable Development Goal 2 (achieve food security for all) requires producing enough food and making food available for all household at all level and at all times, in which agriculture stands as a major pathway doing that. Political stability and absence of violence is required to achieve food security in Nigeria, because crises and insurgency tend to diminish food security; when there is war, people are displaced, one will be left to farm in order to produce food required to maintain a nutritional level (for example, in Nigeria the Fulani herdsmen and Boko Haram insurgency have greatly affected the state of food security in the Northern parts of the country. Farmers have been unable to reap maximum yields from their farmlands because of the destructive nature of cows on their farmlands and violence which have made them to flee from their villages. These have had adverse effect on agricultural produce in Nigeria).

From the result, population components (fertility rate and total population) were observed to be negatively related to food security: 1% change in population leads to 2.1, 28.5 and 41.5% decrease in food security, while fertility rate decrease food security by 66.7, 5.8, 13.8, 78.6 and 30%, respectively. This implies that, increase in population and fertility rate increased the number of households chasing few available produced goods; in this wise, if the agriculture sector is not made efficient to produce enough food for the teaming population, it will definitely lead to food insecurity which is in line with Malthus' theory of population.

Diagnostic tests were used to ensure the validity of the results; for example, *R*-squared measures the goodness of fit. *R*-squared which ranges from 0.50 to 0 89 shows that the model is well fitted as this met the normality criteria for time series variables; *F*-statistic and probability value from the model shows that jointly, the variables are significant in the model; the standard errors were also robust. The result for the second proxy for food security is presented in Table 3.3.

Table 3.3 presents the result for the second proxy for food security which is access to food (GDP per capita). The nutritional aspect of food and nutrition security is achieved when secure access to food is coupled with a sanitary environment, adequate health services and knowledgeable care to ensure a healthy and active life (free from malnutrition) for all household members (FAO 2018). Access to food is ensured when all households have enough resources to obtain food in sufficient quantity, quality and diversity for a nutritious diet. This depends mainly on the amount of household resources and on prices (FAO 2018). Findings presented in Table 3.3 (food access) are similar to the result presented in Table 3.2 (Food availability). The variables are both statistically and economically significant in explaining food access. Agriculture production, employment, value added, access to electricity and political stability were observed to increase food access; population and population growth rate are negatively related to food access.

In summary, in order to ensure the attainment of food security and SDG2 in ECOWAS by 2030, it is good to ensure a sustainable food production systems and implement resilient agricultural practices that increase productivity and production, that help maintain ecosystems, which support capacity for adaptation to climate change, extreme weather, drought, flooding and other disasters and that progressively improve land and soil quality (FAO 2018). By 2030, if the SDG2 is to be attained in this ECOWAS region, the efficiency of the agricultural sector should be enhanced by maintaining the genetic diversity of seeds, cultivated plants and farmed and domesticated animals and their related wild species, including through soundly managed and diversified seed and plant banks at the national, regional and international levels, and promote access to and fair and equitable sharing of benefits arising from the utilisation of genetic resources and associated traditional knowledge.

Also, there should be an increase in investment and credit facilities, including through enhanced international cooperation, in rural infrastructure, agricultural research and extension services, technology development and plant and livestock gene banks in order to enhance agricultural productive capacity among member countries; correct and prevent trade restrictions and distortions in world agricultural markets, including through the parallel elimination of all forms of agricultural export subsidies and all export measures with equivalent effect, adopt measures to ensure the proper functioning of food commodity markets and their derivatives and facilitate timely access to market information, including on food reserves, in order to help limit extreme food price volatility.

Conclusion and Recommendations

This study was motivated by the need of making contribution to research efforts and increase in the frontiers of knowledge of food security in West Africa, which has become a challenge, and it examined the influence of agriculture on food security in the West African sub-region using panel data (2000–2017). The results from descriptive, statistical and econometric analyses confirm that, *inter alia*, agriculture is essential in explaining the rate of food security in West Africa in the quest to attain the SDG2. It was noted that the availability of arable land was one of the major factors to increase food production to counter the plague of food insecurity for the ever-teeming West African population. This is very imperative for sub-region given her abundant land space, which can be adequately cultivated for food production process through active productive means. Thus, the efforts of reducing the rate of food insecurity are essential in this regard. This can also be achieved, among others, by active interactions between government and farmers, to make contribution to important planning issues that relate to food production in West Africa.

Based on the findings of this study the following recommendations are made; first, the governments of the West African countries should ensure that there is adequate security in the economies so as to encourage people to practice agriculture. It was observed from the result of this study that political stability and absence of violence has a significant impact on food access availability (proxy for food security). Second, more people should be encouraged to engage in agricultural activities, this will ensure an increase in agricultural output. Credit facilities (in form of soft loans) should be given to farmers, modern farming equipment should be provided as well as the farmers should also be given fertilizers. Third, social and infrastructural facilities (electricity, pipe borne water, schools, hospitals and good road networks) should be provided in the rural areas. The availability of these amenities in the rural areas will encourage people to remain the villages to practice agriculture, which will in turn increase agricultural output and ensure food security.

References

Afolayan, O., Okodua, H., Matthew, O., & Osabohien, R. (2019). Reducing Unemployment Malaise in Nigeria: The Role of Electricity Consumption and Human Capital. *International Journal of Energy Economics and Policy, 9*(4), 63–73.

Atinmo, T., & Adeniran, T. (1999). Policy Failure in the Search for Food Security in Nigeria. *European Journal of Sustainable Development, 1*(2), 199–220.

Bamisaye, A. (1987). Food Crisis and Its Implication in Political Transformation of Nigeria Since Independence. In S. O. Olugbemi (Ed.), *Alternative Political Futures for Nigeria*. Lagos, Nigeria: A Publication of the Nigerian Political Publication.

Barrett, C. B., & Palm, C. (2016). Meeting the Global Food Security Challenge: Obstacles and Opportunities Ahead. *Global Food Security, 100*(11), 1–4.

Benson, T. (2008). *Improving Nutrition as a Development Priority: Addressing Under Nutrition in National Policy Processes in Sub-Saharan Africa* (Research Report No. 156). Washington, DC: International Food Policy Research Institute.

Chen, S., & Kates, W. (1994). World Food Security: Prospects and Trends. *Journal of World Food Policy, 19*(2), 192–208.

Collinson, M. A., White, M. J., Ginsburg, C., Gomez-Olive, F. Xavier, Kahn, K., & Tollman, S. (2016). Youth Migration, Livelihood Prospects and Demographic Dividend: A Comparison of the Census 2011 and Agincourt Health and Surveillance System in the Rural Northeast of South Africa. *African Population Studies, 30*(2), 2629–2639.

Di Falco, S., Yesuf, M., Kohlin, G., & Ringler, C. (2011). Estimating the Impact of Climate Change on Agriculture in Low-Income Countries: Household Level Evidence from the Nile Basin. *Ethiopia Environmental and Resource Economics, 52*, 457–478.

Diao, X., Hazell, P., & Thurlow, J. (2009). The Role of Agriculture in African Development. *World Development, 38*(10), 1375–1383.

Ejemeyovwi, J. O., Osabuohien, E. S., & Osabohien, R. (2018). ICT Investments, Human Capital Development and Institutions in ECOWAS. *International Journal of Economics and Business Research, 15*(4), 463–474.

Eliamoni, L., Fenggying, N., & Cheng, F. (2015). The Role of Agriculture in the Economic Growth and Poverty Reduction in Tanzania. *Journal of Economics and Sustainable Development, 6*(14), 154–165.

Fasoyiro, S., & Taiwo, K. (2012). Strategies for Increasing Food Production and Food Security in Nigeria. *Journal of Agricultural Food Information, 13*(4), 338–355.

Fawole, W. O., Ilbasmis, E., & Ozkan, B. (2015, September 30 and October 3). *Food Insecurity in Africa in Terms of Causes, Effects and Solutions: A Case Study of Nigeria*. A Paper Presentation at the 2nd International Conference on Sustainable Agriculture and Environment held at the Selcuk University and Bahri Dagdas International Agricultural Research Institute Campus in the City of Konya, Turkey.

Food and Agriculture Organisation (FAO). (2017). *World Agriculture: Towards 2015/2030* (FAO Corporate Document Repository, pp. 4–8).

Food and Agricultural Organisation (FAO). (2018). Tackling Poverty and Hunger Through Digital Innovation.

Greene, W. H. (2008). Econometric Analysis, (6th Ed.). *Upper Saddle River*. N. J: Prentice-Hall.

Gustavo, A., & Kostas, S. (2007). Rural Development and Poverty Reduction: Is Agriculture Still the Key? *Journal of Agricultural and Development Economics, 4*(1), 5–46.

IFPRI. (2005). *The Role of Nigerian Agriculture in West African Food Security, Report on Nigeria Strategy Support Program*. Retrieved on June 25, 2019 from http://nssp.ifpri.info/2012/08/05/the-role-of-nigerian-agriculture-in-west-african-food-security/.

Lam, V. W. Y., Cheung, W. W. L., Swartz, W., & Sumaila, U. R. (2012). Climate Change Impacts on Fisheries in West Africa: Implications for Economic, Food, and Nutritional Security. *African Journal of Marine Science, 34*, 103–117.

Love, I., & Zicchino, L. (2006). Financial Development and Dynamic Investment Behavior: Evidence from Panel VAR. *Quarterly Review of Economics and Finance, 46*(2), 190–210.

Matthew, O., Ede, C., Osabohien, R., Ejemeyovwi, J., Fasina, F., & Akinpelumi, D. (2018a). Electricity Consumption and Human Capital Development in Nigeria: Exploring the Implications for Economic Growth. *International Journal of Energy Economics and Policy, 8*(6), 1–8.

Matthew, O. A., Miebaka-Ogan, T., Popoola, O., Olawande, T., Osabohien, R., Urhie, E., et al. (2019). Electricity Consumption, Government Expenditure and Sustainable Development in Nigeria: A Co-integration Approach. *International Journal of Energy Economics and Policy, 9*(4), 74–80.

Matthew, O., Osabohien, R., Fagbeminiyi, F., & Fasina, A. (2018b). Greenhouse Gas Emissions and Health Outcomes in Nigeria: Empirical Insight from ARDL Technique. *International Journal of Energy Economics and Policy, 8*(3), 43–50.

Nellemann, C., & MacDevette, M. (Eds.). (2009). *The Environmental, Food Crisis: The Environment's Role in Averting Future Food Crises: A UNEP Rapid Response Assessment*. UNEP/EarthPrint.

Obayelu, E. (2015). Transformation from Subsistence to Commercial Agriculture in Nigeria: The Effects of Large-Scale Land Acquisition on Smallholder Farmers. In E. Osabuohien (Ed.), *Handbook of Research on In-Country Determinants and Implications of Foreign Land Acquisitions* (pp. 409–431). Hershey, PA: Business Science.

Ogbalubi, L. N., & Wokocha, C. C. (2013). Agricultural Development and Employment Generation: The Nigerian Experience. *Journal of Agriculture and Veterinary Science, 2*(2), 60–69.

Olofin, O. P., Olufolahan, T. J., & Jooda, T. D. (2015). Food Security, Income Growth and Government Effectiveness in West African Countries. *European Scientific Journal November, 11*(31), 417–429.

Osabohien, R., Afolabi, A., & Godwin, A. (2018a). Agricultural Credit Facility and Food Security in Nigeria: An Analytic Review. *The Open Agriculture Journal, 12,* 227–239.

Osabohien, R., Matthew, O., Aderounmu, B., & Olawande, T. (2019). Greenhouse Gas Emissions and Crop Production in West Africa: Examining the Mitigating Potential of Social Protection, *International Journal of Energy Economics and Policy, 9*(1), 57–66.

Osabohien, R., Osabuohien, E., & Urhie, E. (2018b). Food Security, Institutional Framework and Technology: Examining the Nexus in Nigeria Using ARDL Approach. *Current Nutrition and Food Science, 14*(2), 154–163.

Osabohien, R., Osuagwu, E., Osabuohien, E., Ekhator-Mobayode, U. E., Matthew, O., & Gershon, O. (2020). Household Access to Agricultural Credit and Agricultural Production in Nigeria: A Propensity Score Matching Model. *South African Journal of Economic and Management Sciences, 23*(1), a2688. https://doi.org/10.4102/sajems.v23i1.2688.

Osuma, G., Ikpefan, A., Osabohien, R., Ndigwe, C., & Nkwodimmah, P. (2018). Working Capital Management and Bank Performance: Empirical Research of Ten Deposit Money Banks in Nigeria. *Banks and Bank Systems, 13*(2), 49–61.

Pearce, D., Cline, W., Achanta, A., Fankhauser, S., Pachauri, R., Tol, R., et al. (1996). The Social Cost of Climate Change: Greenhouse Damage and the Benefits of Control. In *Climate Change 1995: Economic and Social Dimensions of Climate Change*. Intergovernmental Panel on Climate Change. Cambridge, UK: Cambridge University Press.

Regional Agricultural Policy for West Africa—ECOWAP. (2008, December 9). *Working Paper Developed for the Paris Conference.*

Schmidhuber, J., & Tubiello, F. N. (2007). Global Food Security Under Climate Change. *PNAS, 104,* 19703–19708.

Sen, A., & Drèze, J. (1989). *Hunger and Public Action*. Oxford: Clarendon Press.

Swallow, B. (2005). Potential for Poverty Reduction Strategies to address Community Priorities: Case Study of Kenya. *World Development, 33*(2), 301–332.

Tol, R. (2002a). New Estimates of the Damage Costs of Climate Change, Part I: Benchmark Estimates. *Environmental & Resource Economics, 21*, 47–73.

Tol, R. (2002b). New Estimates of the Damage Costs of Climate Change, Part II: Dynamic Estimates. *Environmental & Resource Economics, 21*, 135–160.

CHAPTER 4

Effect of Infrastructural Growth on Agricultural Research and Development in Nigeria

Samuel Sesan Abolarin, Joseph Chinedu Umeh, and Celina Biam

Introduction

Extensive empirical evidence demonstrates that investments in agricultural research and development (R&D) have greatly contributed to economic growth, agricultural development and poverty reduction in Sub-Saharan Africa (SSA) over the past five decades (World Bank 2007; IAASTD 2008). Government appears to be investing heavily in R&D and the main impetus leading many governments in developing countries of the world to increase their expenditures on R&D in critical sectors of their economies is the realization that the fate of modern economy is determined mainly by growth in the efficiency of labour (Pessoa 2007). New technologies resulting from R&D investments have enhanced the quantity and quality of agricultural output, and have led to higher incomes,

S. S. Abolarin (✉) · J. C. Umeh · C. Biam
Department of Agricultural Economics, University of Agriculture, Makurdi, Nigeria

G. Odularu (ed.), *Nutrition, Sustainable Agriculture and Climate Change in Africa*,
https://doi.org/10.1007/978-3-030-47875-9_4

greater food security and better nutrition. Given important challenges, such as rapid population growth, adaptation to climate change, water scarcity, and the volatility of prices in global markets, investing in agricultural R&D remain crucial in increasing agricultural productivity and reduced poverty (Beintema and Stads 2011).

Research shows that productivity increase in agriculture, which is an effective driver of economic growth and poverty reduction, depends on good rural infrastructure, well-functioning domestic markets, appropriate institutions and access to appropriate technology (Andersen and Shimokawa 2007). Infrastructural development, like other public investments, raises agricultural productivity, which in turn induces growth in the rural areas, bringing about higher agricultural wages and improved opportunities for non-farm labour. The rise in agricultural productivity, which reduces food prices, benefits both urban and rural inhabitants who are net food buyers. Thus, aside from its growth benefits, agricultural productivity has significant poverty reduction effects. Infrastructure contributes to economic development both by increasing productivity and providing amenities which enhance the quality of life (Llanto 2012).

The contribution of rural infrastructure fosters physical connectivity and promotes better integration of rural and agricultural areas with growing urban markets, which, in turn, are linked to the global trading markets, thereby stimulating economic growth and creating poverty reduction opportunities in those areas (Llanto 2012). The flow of infrastructure services is the main measure of economic benefits from these sectors, and that an efficient allocation of resources in this area should be in response to effective demand for services (Edame 2014). Development economists have long acknowledged the centrality of public expenditure, particularly on infrastructure as an important instrument in the development process. Public expenditure has remained a central issue in economic development, especially developing countries in Sub-Saharan Africa, whose economies are characterized by structural rigidities, weak support services and institutional framework, declining productivity, high level corruption cum policy instability. This gloomy picture has led to researches aimed at investigating whether public expenditure on infrastructure has yielded significant results over time (Edame 2009). Therefore, this study analyzed the effect of infrastructural growth on agricultural R&D in Nigeria (1981–2013).

Methodology

The study area: The study area is Nigeria. Nigeria lies between latitude and longitude of 4^0 to 14^0N and 2^0 to 15^0E, respectively

Methods of Data Collection Techniques: Secondary data were used to carry out this study. Augmented Dickey-Fuller was used to determine the stationarity of variables of interest. Johansen co-integration test was used to assess the existence of the long-run relationship between infrastructural growth and R&D; Vector Error Correction Model (VECM) was used to analyze long- and short-run effects of infrastructural growth on R&D. Granger causality test was used to determine the direction of causality.

Model Specification

Unit Root Test

Following Edame and Fonta (2014), The Augmented Dickey-Fuller (ADF) test assumes that the data generating process is a first-order autoregressive (AR1) process, and if this is not, the autocorrelation in the error term biases the test. The ADF is used to avoid such bias in the test since it includes the first difference in lags in such a way that the error term is distributed as white noise. The test formula for the DF and ADF are shown in Eqs. (4.1) and (4.2), respectively. Augmented Dickey-Fuller can be defined as:

$$\Delta Y_t = \alpha + \rho Y_{t-1} + \varepsilon_t \tag{4.1}$$

$$\Delta Y_t = \alpha + \rho Y_{t-1} + \Sigma \gamma \Delta Y_{t-j} + \varepsilon_t \tag{4.2}$$

Here the significance of ρ would be tested against the null that $\rho = 0$. Thus if the hypothesis of non stationary cannot be rejected, the variables are differenced until they become stationary, that is until the existence of a unit root is rejected. We then proceed to test for co-integration (Edame and Fonta 2014).

Johansen Co-Integration Test

A linear combination of two or more $I(1)$ series may be stationary or $I(0)$, in which case the series are co-integrated. The null hypothesis for the Johansen Co-integration test ($H!{:}r\ = 0$) implies that co-integration does not exist, while the alternative hypothesis ($H!{:}r > 0$) implies that it does. If the null for non-co-integration is rejected, the lagged residual from the co-integrating regression is imposed as the error correction term in a Vector Error Correction Model (VECM) given below as:

$$\nabla Y_t = \prod Y_{t-1} + \sum_{i=1}^{k-1} \tau_i \nabla Y_{t-1} + u + \varepsilon_t \tag{4.3}$$

Where:

$\nabla Y_t =$	First difference of a $(n \times i)$ vector of the n variables of interest
$\prod = (n \times n)$	Coefficient matrix associated with lagged values of the endogenous dependent variables
$Y_{t-1} =$	Lagged values of Y_t
$\tau = (n \times (k-1))$	Matrix of short-term coefficients
$u = (n \times 1)$	Vector of constant
$\varepsilon_t = (n \times 1)$	Vector of White Noise Residuals

Equation for Long-Run Relationship

The model for the long-term effect of infrastructure on agricultural R&D is given explicitly as:

$$\text{lnAR\&DEX}_t = a_0 + a_1\text{lnRDS}_t + a_2\text{lnETS}_t + a_3\text{lnWRS}_t + u_t \tag{4.4}$$

AR&D =	Agricultural Research & Development (million naira)
$\text{RDS}_t =$	Road construction (million naira)
$\text{ETSL}_t =$	Electricity supply (million naira)
$\text{WRS}_t =$	Water supply (million naira)
Ln =	Natural Logarithm
$\nabla =$	difference operator

A priori expectation: The coefficients of expenditure on Roads construction (RDS_t), expenditure on electricity supply (ETSL_t), expenditure on Water supply (WRS_t) are expected to be positive.

Equation for Short-Run Relationship

The model for the short-term effect of infrastructure on R&D was given explicitly as:

$$\nabla \text{lnAR\&DEX}_t = a_0 + \sum_{i=1}^{p} a_1 \nabla \text{lnRDS}_{t-i} + \sum_{i=1}^{p} a_2 \nabla \text{lnETS}_{t-i} + \sum_{i-1}^{p} a_3 \nabla \text{lnWRS}_{t-i} + \varepsilon_t \qquad (4.5)$$

Where

AR&DEX =	Research and Development Expenditure (million naira)
RDS_t =	Road construction (million naira)
ETS_t =	Electricity supply (million naira)
WRS_t =	Water supply (million naira)
Ln =	Natural Logarithm
∇ =	difference operator

A priori expectation: The coefficients of Research and Development Expenditure on Roads construction (RDS_t), electricity supply (ETS_t) and Water supply (WRS_t) are expected to be positive.

Granger Causality Test

Causality between infrastructure and AR&D was given as:

$$\text{R\&DEX}_t = \alpha o + \sum_{i=l}^{p} \alpha_i \text{R\&DEX}_{t-i} + \sum_{i=l}^{p} \theta_i \text{RDS}_{t-i} + \varepsilon_{1t} \qquad (4.6)$$

$$\text{RDS}_t = \beta o + \sum_{i=l}^{p} \beta_i \text{RDS}_{t-i} + \sum_{i=l}^{p} \varphi_i \text{R\&DEX}_{t-i} + \varepsilon_{2t} \qquad (4.7)$$

$$\text{AR\&DEX}_t = \alpha o + \sum_{i=l}^{p} \lambda_i \text{R\&DEX}_{t-i} + \sum_{i=l}^{p} \mu_i \text{WRS}_{t-i} + u_{1t} \qquad (4.8)$$

$$\text{WRS}_t = \beta o + \sum_{i=l}^{p} \delta_i \text{WRS}_{t-i} + \sum_{i=l}^{p} \gamma_i \text{R\&DEX}_{t-i} + u_{2t} \qquad (4.9)$$

$$\text{R\&DEX}_t = \alpha o + \sum_{i=l}^{p} \psi_i \text{R\&DEX}_{t-i} + \sum_{i=l}^{p} \vartheta_i \text{ETS}_{t-i} + v_{1t} \quad (4.10)$$

$$\text{ETS}_t = \beta o + \sum_{i=l}^{p} \sigma_i \text{ETS}_{t-i} + \sum_{i=l}^{p} \pi_i \text{R\&DEX}_{t-i} + v_{2t} \quad (4.11)$$

where the variables are as defined previously. For the purpose of illustration, assume that $\text{AR\&DEX}_t$ and WRS_t are to be tested for causality. In this VAR, if the θ_i in Eq. (4.8) is significant and φ_i in Eq. (4.9) is not significant; then there exists a unidirectional causality running from WRS_t to $\text{R\&DEX}_t$. The opposite is true when φ_i is significant in Eq. (4.9) with insignificant θ_i in Eq. (4.8), that is there is unidirectional causality running from $\text{R\&DEX}_t$ to WRS_t. In case both φ_i and θ_i in Eqs. (4.9) and (4.8) are significant then there exists a bi-directional causation. However if the two coefficients in the two equations are insignificant then existence of any causation between the two variables is rejected.

Result and Discussion

Augmented Dickey-Fuller (ADF) Unit Root Tests

The results of the unit root tests are presented in Table 4.1. The null hypothesis of the presence of unit root (non-stationarity) was tested against the alternative hypothesis of the absence of a unit root (stationarity). The result indicates that agricultural research & development expenditure (AR&DEX), road constructions (RDS),water supply (WRS) and electricity supply (ETS) were not stationary at their levels as shown by

Table 4.1 Results of Augmented Dickey-Fuller (ADF) Unit root tests

Variables	*ADF*	*Levels*	*ADF*	*1ST Diff.*	*Decision*
D(LGRDS)	−0.732	−2.956	−4.362	−2.963	I(1)
D(LGWRS)	−0.450	−2.959	−6.268	−2.963	I(1)
D(LGETS)	−0.226	−2.959	−3.594	−2.963	I(1)
D(LGAR&DEX)	−1.453	−2.963	−3.919	−2.967	I(1)

Source Author's creation based on Eview

Table 4.2 Co-integrations test between infrastructural growth and agricultural R&D expenditure (R&DEX)

Hypothesized no. of CE(s)	*Eigen value*	*Likelihood ratio*	*0.05 Critical value*	*0.01 Critical value*
None**	0.6809	54.4967	47.21	54.46
At most 1	0.4352	25.9400	29.68	35.65
At most 2	0.3726	11.6597	15.41	20.04
At most 3	0.0002	0.0042	3.76	6.65

Note **Existence of 1 co-integrating equation. Long-run relationship between infrastructural growth and agricultural R&D expenditure (R&DEX)
Source Author's creation based on Eview

the Augmented Dickey-Fuller (ADF) statistics which are lower in absolute terms than the standard critical values (10, 5 and 1%). However, these variables were found to be stationary on first differencing.

Johansen Co-Integration Test Between Infrastructural Growth and Agricultural R&D Expenditure (R&DEX)

Table 4.2 shows the result of Johansen co-integration tests. The tests are based on the Maximum Eigen value of the stochastic matrix as well as the Likelihood Ratio tests which is in turn based on the trace of the stochastic matrix. From the results, it is evident that maximum Eigen value test indicates one co-integrating equation between infrastructural growth and research and development expenditure as the value of likelihood ratio is greater than the critical value at 0.01. Thus, we concluded that there is a unique long-run equilibrium relationship between effects of infrastructural growth on research and development expenditure in Nigeria.

Long-Run Relationship Between Infrastructural Growth and Agricultural R&D Expenditure (R&DEX)

Table 4.3 shows the estimated effect of infrastructural growth on research and development expenditure in the long run. The result showed that the expenditure on road constructions in the previous year, expenditure on water supply in the previous year and expenditure on electricity supply

Table 4.3 Effect of infrastructural growth on agricultural R&D expenditure (R&DEX) in the long-run

Variables	*R&DEX model*
RDS_{t-1}	0.831583
	(15.1049)***
WRS_{t-1}	−0.0067
	−(3.2988)***
ETS_{t-1}	0.7615
	(3.9886)***
Trend	−0.1542
	−(17.4453)***
Constant	4.33959
R-square	0.551962
Adj. R-square	0.283139
Sum of sq. resids	0.366728
S.E equation	0.156360
F-statistic	2.053254
Log-likelihood	17.30168
Akaike A/C	−0.584134
Schwarz SC	−0.096584
Mean dependent	−0.023328
S.D. dependent	0.184675

Note ***significant at 1%. Figure in parenthesis are the t-ratio
Source Author's creation based on Eview

in the previous year have significant effect on research and development in the long run. Specifically, the co efficient of expenditure on roads construction in the previous year and expenditure on electricity supply in the previous year are positive and significant at 1% level of probability, implying that a unit increase in expenditure on road construction in the previous year and expenditure on electricity supply in the previous year will increase research and development by 0.83 and 0.76, respectively. This may be due to the fact that road and electricity are important infrastructures which reduce transaction cost for agricultural market, R&D and the dissemination of agricultural technology through extension to increase agricultural productivity. This result is in agreement with similar and previous studies which analyzed the effect of public expenditure on levels of rural poverty across Indian and Uganda, and found out that, spending on road infrastructure generates the second highest agricultural productivity returns after spending on agricultural research; also, increase in electricity supply in the previous year will improve the quality of research activities carried-out.

Table 4.4 Short run effect of infrastructural growth on agricultural R&D expenditure (R&DEX)

Variable	*D(LGR&DEX)*	*D(LGRDS)*	*D(WRS)*	*D(ETS)*
ECM I	−0.3199	−2.8107	2.4022	0.1409
	−(1.3246)	−(5.0076)	(2.04323)**	(0)
D(LGR&DEX(−1))	0.1959	1.7911	−0.7799	0.4702
	(0.6392)	(2.5154)**	−(0.5227)	(2.0207)**
D(LGR&DEX(−2))	−0.5796	0.2495	−2.0336	−0.2018
	−(2.1968)**	(0.4068)	−(1.5827)	−(1.0073)
D(LGRDS(−1))	−0.1237	−1.2266	0.8699	0.1274
	−(0.8479)	−(3.6178)***	(1.2244)	(1.1994)
D(LGRDS(−2))	0.0323	−0.7055	0.9064	0.1197
	(0.2849)	−(2.6760)***	(1.6407)*	(1.3889)
D(LGWRS(−1))	−0.1362	−0.03676	0.1891	−0.0272
	−(3.1796)***	−(0.3693)	(0.9065)	−(0.8346)
D(LGWRS(−2))	−0.0132	−0.0121	0.4065	0.0002
	−(0.3142)	−(0.1233)	(1.985)**	(0.0049)
D(LGETS(−1))	−0.1208	−1.0121	0.3983	0.2458
	−(0.3539)	−(1.2756)	(0.2396)	(0.9479)
D(LGETS(−2))	0.6711	0.1635	1.3402	0.1465
	(2.1554)**	(0.2259)	(0.8838)	(0.6193)
C	−0.0030	0.1739	−0.6175	−0.0808
	−(0.0510)	(1.2570)	−(2.1293)	−(1.7859)
R-square	0.5519	0.6752	0.5511	0.3234
Adj. R-squ	0.2831	0.4804	0.2818	−0.0826
Sum of sq. resids	0.3667	1.9810	8.6988	0.2116
S.E equation	0.1564	0.3634	0.7615	0.1188
F-statistic	2.0533	3.4654	2.0463	0.7965
Log-likelihood	17.3017	−3.7826	−22.2774	24.1786
Akaike A/C	−0.5841	1.1026	2.5822	−1.1343
Schwarz SC	−0.0966	1.5902	3.0697	−0.6467
Mean dependent	0.0233	0.1989	0.1546	0.0327
S.D. dependent	0.1847	0.5042	0.8986	0.1141

Note ***, **, * significant at 1, 5 and 10% respectively. Figure in parenthesis are the *t*-ratio
Source Author's creation based on Eview

Furthermore, electricity supply will enhance the performance of the research staff. This result is in agreement with Llanto (2012) on impact of infrastructure on agricultural productivity; the author found that access to electricity increase efficiency and creates various income earning opportunities for rural households. In contrast, the coefficient of expenditure on water supply in the previous year is negative and significant at 1% level of probability, implying that a unit increased in expenditure on water supply in the previous year reduces Agricultural R&D expenditure by −0.006. This implies that, a unit increase in expenditure on water supply reduces R&D expenditure.

Short-Run Relationship Between Infrastructural Growth and Agricultural R&D (R&DEX)

The result of estimated effect of infrastructural growth on agricultural research and development expenditures (R&DEX) in the short run is presented in Table 4.5. The result shows that the coefficient of R&D expenditure two years ago, the coefficient of water supply expenditure in the previous year and coefficient of electricity supply expenditure two years ago have significant effect on research and development expenditure in the short run. Specifically, the coefficient of research and development expenditure two years ago is negative and significant at 5% level of probability, implying that a unit increase in the coefficient of research and development expenditure two years ago reduces research and development expenditure by −0.58 in the short run. Similarly, the coefficient of water supply expenditure in the previous year was negative and significant at 1% level of probability. This implies that a unit increase in expenditure on water supply in the previous year reduces the expenditure of research and development by −0.14. This result is against Rosegrant et al. (1998) on output response to prices and public investment on agriculture in Indonesian who found that the impacts of investments in irrigation are positive, whereas the coefficients on research and extension are not statistically significant. In contrast, the coefficient of expenditure on electricity supply two years ago was positive and significant at 5% level of probability, implying that unit increase in electricity supply two years ago increases research and development expenditure by 0.67. This is attributed to the fact that electricity increase efficiency/performance of researchers carrying out research activities. This result is in agreement with Llanto (2012) who found that access to electricity increase efficiency and creates various income earning opportunities for rural households. Furthermore, the coefficient of research and development expenditure in the previous year, coefficient of roads construction expenditure in the previous year and coefficient of roads construction expenditure two years ago have significant effect on roads construction expenditure in the short run. Specifically, a unit increase in the coefficient of agricultural

Table 4.5 Granger causality test between infrastructural growth and agricultural research and development

Hypothesis	X^2 *cal*	X^2 *tab*	*Decision*
AR&D expenditure in the previous year does not Granger cause AR&D expenditure	0.4471	16.274	Accepted
AR&D expenditure two year ago does not Granger cause AR&D expenditure	5.1619	16.274	Accepted
AR&D expenditure in the previous year does not Granger cause roads supply	9.5353	16.274	Accepted
AR&D expenditure two year ago does not granger cause roads supply	0.2277	16.274	Accepted
AR&D expenditure in the previous year does not Granger cause water supply	0.8815	16.274	Accepted
AR&D expenditure two year ago does not Granger cause water supply	6.6405	16.274	Accepted
AR&D expenditure in the previous year does not Granger cause electricity supply	4.3043	16.274	Accepted
AR&D expenditure two year ago does not Granger cause electricity supply	1.0554	16.274	Accepted
Roads supply in the previous year does not Granger cause AR&D expenditure	0.7342	16.274	Accepted
Roads supply two years ago does not Granger cause AR&D expenditure	0.0822	16.274	Accepted
Roads supply in the previous year does not Granger cause roads supply	14.59	16.274	Accepted
Roads supply two years does not Granger cause roads supply	7.66	16.274	Accepted
Roads supply in the previous year does not Granger cause water supply	2.26	16.274	Accepted
Roads supply two years does not Granger cause water supply	3.51		Accepted
Roads supply in the previous year does not Granger cause electricity supply	1.34	16.274	Accepted
Roads supply two years does not Granger cause electricity supply	1.94	16.274	Accepted
Water supply in the previous year does not Granger cause AR&D expenditure	10.13	16.274	Accepted
Water supply two years ago does not Granger cause AR&D expenditure	0.099	16.274	Accepted
Water supply in the previous year does not Granger cause roads supply	7.66	16.274	Accepted

(continued)

Table 4.5 (continued)

Hypothesis	X^2 *cal*	X^2 *tab*	*Decision*
Water supply two years ago does not Granger cause roads supply	0.27	16.274	Accepted
Water supply in the previous year does not Granger cause water supply	0.88	16.274	Accepted
Water supply two years ago does not Granger cause water supply	4.12		Accepted
Water supply in the previous year does not Granger cause electricity supply	0.69	16.274	Accepted
Water supply two years ago does not Granger cause electricity supply	0.004	16.274	Accepted
Electricity supply in the previous year does not Granger cause AR&D expenditure	0.14	16.274	Accepted
Electricity supply two years ago does not Granger cause AR&D expenditure	5.09	16.274	Accepted
Electricity supply in the previous does not Granger cause roads supply	2.65	16.274	Accepted
Electricity supply two years ago does not Granger cause roads supply	0.08	16.274	Accepted
Electricity supply in the previous does not Granger cause water supply	0.22	16.274	Accepted
Electricity supply two years ago does not Granger cause water supply	2.58	16.274	Accepted
Electricity supply in the previous does not Granger cause electricity supply	0.96	16.274	Accepted
Electricity supply two years ago does not Granger cause electricity supply	0.41	16.274	Accepted

Source Author's creation based on Eview

R&D expenditure in the previous year increases expenditure on roads construction by 1.79 at 5% level of probability; this implies that access to good roads increases efficiency and safe transportation cost. This result is against Fan et al. (1999) on the effect of public expenditure on levels of rural poverty across Indian states where a clear distinction was made between expenditure on rural education, targeted rural development, public health, irrigation, power generation, agricultural R&D and rural roads. The author result showed that agricultural R&D, rural roads, rural education and targeted rural development expenditure all have negative and statistically significant effects on agricultural productivity.

However, the coefficient of roads expenditure in the previous year and two years ago are negative and significant, implying that unit increase in the coefficient of road construction expenditure in the previous year and two years ago reduces expenditure on roads construction by −1.23 and −0.71 at 1% level of probability, respectively in the short run. This was attributed to limited investment in rural roads in Nigeria. This result is in agreement with Idachaba (2006) who found that both urban and rural infrastructure have witnessed monumental decay in Nigeria, and several rural communities have been cut off due to poor and inaccessible roads.

The coefficient of road construction expenditure and the coefficient of water supply expenditure two years ago have significant effects on water supply expenditure in the short run. Specifically, the coefficient of roads construction expenditure and coefficient of water supply expenditure are positive and significant at 1 and 5% level of probability, respectively implying that unit increase on roads construction expenditure and water supply two years ago will increase expenditure on water supply by 0.91 and 0.41, respectively. This may be due to the fact that access to good roads may promote transportation of water from one rural area to the other. This result is in agreement with Abubakar (2008) that rural roads play a major role in facilitating and enabling access to socioeconomic centres in rural areas and ultimately contributes to agricultural productivity and achieving equity in a country. The coefficient of research and development expenditure in the previous year were positive and significant on electricity supply expenditure at 5% level of probability, implying that unit increase in the coefficient of R&D expenditure in the previous year will increase expenditure on electricity supply by 0.47. This may be attributed to the fact that electricity is an important infrastructure in carrying out research activities. This result is in agreement with Llanto

(2012) who found that access to electricity increase efficiency and creates various income earning opportunities for rural households.

Table 4.4 shows that there was no causality between the variables of infrastructural growth and Research and Development within the period under investigation. This may be due to inconsistency in infrastructure, government instability and high level of corruption during the period under review.

Conclusion and Recommendations

The study examined the effect of infrastructural growth on AR&D in Nigeria (1981–2013). It was found that infrastructural growth has significant effects on agricultural research and development (AR&D) both at the long and short run, respectively in Nigeria. Based on the study, the result revealed that there was no causality between infrastructural growth and agricultural research and development expenditure. It was recommended that government through Federal Ministry of Works and Housing (FMW&H) in conjunction with Federal Ministry of Agriculture and Rural Development (FMARD) should provide adequate and quality infrastructure in rural areas. Targeted programmes towards rural infrastructural development most especially rural roads, electrifications and adequate quality water supply should be provided by allocating major part of government budget to rural infrastructure. Finally, the study also found that, there is no causality between infrastructural growth and agricultural research and development during the period under review. It was recommended that:

i. Policy measures should be put in place by federal ministry of works in order to improve on the existing infrastructures in Nigeria in order to drive research and development activities in Nigeria
ii. Targeted programmes towards rural infrastructural development most especially rural roads, electrifications and adequate water supply should be formulated by allocating major part of government budget to rural infrastructure.
iii. Efficient and effective allocations of adequate resources should be made to infrastructure investment that will lead to growth in the production and flow of infrastructure services. This remains one of the main measures of economic benefits from these sectors,

therefore, efficient allocation of resources in the area should be in response to effective demand for services.

iv. With the past performance of agricultural R&D, government should commit a significant proportion of its resources for developing appropriate technologies.

References

Abubakar, S. (2008). *The Impact of Rural Infrastructure on Social Development in Giwa Local Government Area, Kaduna State, Nigeria*. Being A Thesis Submitted to the Schools of Postgraduate Studies Ahmadu Bello University Zaria, In Partial Fulfillment of the Requirements for the Degree of Master's in Science Geography.

Andersen, P., & Shimokawa, S. (2007, May 29–30). *Rural Infrastructure and Agricultural Development*. Paper presented at the Annual Bank Conference on Development Economics, Tokyo, Japan.

Beintema, N. M., & Stads, G. J. (2011). *African Agricultural R&D in the New Millennium: Progress for Some, Challenges for Many* (pp. 1–44). Food Policy Report. Washington, DC: International Food Policy Research Institute.

Edame, G. E. (2009). *"Determinants of Public Expenditure on Infrastructure and Economic Growth in Nigeria, 1970–2006": A Co-integration and Error Correction Specification* (An Unpublished Ph.D Thesis, Department of Economics, pp. 47–67). University of Nigeria, Nsukka.

Edame, G. E. (2014). Trends Analysis of Public Expenditure on Infrastructure and Economic Growth In Nigeria. *International Journal of Asian Social Science, 4*(4), 480–491.

Edame, G. E., & Fonta, W. M. (2014). The Impact of Government Expenditure on Infrastructure in Nigeria: A Co-integration & Error Correction Specification. *International Journal of African and Asian Studies, 3*, 50–63.

Fan, S., Hazell, P., & Thorat, S. (1999). *Linkages Between Government Spending, Growth and Poverty in Rural China* (Research Report 125). Washington, DC: IFPRT.

Idachaba, F. S. (2006). *Rural Development in Nigeria: Foundation of Sustainable Economic Recovery* (p. 12). Ile-Ife: Obafemi Awolowo University.

International Assessment of Agricultural Knowledge, Science and Technology for Development. (IAASTD). (2008). *Synthesis Report* (pp. 78:177–180). Washington, DC: Island Press.

Llanto, G. M. (2012). *The Impact of Infrastructure on Agricultural Productivity* (Discussion Paper Series No. 2012–12). Philippine Institute for Development Studies.

Pessoa, A. (2007). *Innovation and Economic Growth: What Is the Actual Importance of R&D* (FEP Working paper 254). Universidade de Economia do Porto. *Jel Codes: 030, 032, 033, 038.*

Rosegrant, M., Kasryno, F., & Perez, N. D. (1998). Output Response to Prices and Public Investment in Agriculture: Indonesian Food Crops. *Perez Journal of Development Economics, 55*(2), 333–352.

World Bank. (2007). *World Development Report 2008: Agriculture for Development* (pp. 68–99). Washington, DC.

CHAPTER 5

Sustainable Seeds Supply, Public Infrastructure, Research and Development (R&D) Expenditures in Nigeria

Donald Denen Dzever, Ugochukwu Christopher Nnama, and Ayuba Ali

Introduction

Around the world, researchers, policy makers, and private sectors are working hard to improve seed provision to farmers in developing countries in order to increase agricultural productivity, nutrition, and rural well-being. Between 2007 and 2012, for example, 50% of the World Bank's 191 projects promoting sustainable agriculture, totaling $513m, had a seed system component (Rajalahti 2013). The Alliance for Green Revolution in Africa (AGRA) has placed particular emphasis on strengthening the seed sector and promoting the commercialization, distribution, and adoption of improved crop varieties (AGRA 2013). Many development donors have projects, some spanning more than a decade, aimed at improving farmer access to adapted and certified seed, as well

D. D. Dzever (✉) · U. C. Nnama · A. Ali
Department of Agricultural Economics, Federal University of Agriculture Makurdi, Makurdi, Nigeria

G. Odularu (ed.), *Nutrition, Sustainable Agriculture and Climate Change in Africa*,
https://doi.org/10.1007/978-3-030-47875-9_5

as supporting the informal seed sector (Food Agriculture and Natural Resources Policy Analysis Network [FANRPAN] 2010; Gill et al. 2013). In addition, a diverse array of donors and NGOs invest considerable effort in supporting community-based initiatives that assist farmers in seed enterprises, seed production, and seed sharing (Kugbei et al. 2000; Gyawali 2010; Tin et al. 2011; Lacoste et al. 2012).

Agribusiness refers to the generic term for the various businesses involved in the food production chain, including farming (both subsistence and mechanized farming), seed supply, manure, fertilizers and agro-chemicals, farm machinery, distribution, wholesale and retail sales, processing, research and development, marketing and financing of the agro-allied industry (Pawa 2013). The nature and character of farm agribusiness linkages in Nigeria can best be understood within the context of the Nigerian economy. Obviously, the supply of raw materials to the agro-industrial processing and manufacturing sector is a primary role of agriculture. This role also facilitates the other traditional roles of agriculture as a food supplier, provider of employment opportunities and income generation, and a contributor to foreign exchange earnings through exports. In Nigeria, the rate of achievement of the linkage between agriculture and industrial sector has remained very tardy. This is partly because of the frequent changes in policy beginning with the import substitution strategies of the pre-1986 era that discouraged industrialists from patronizing locally produced raw materials (Idachaba 2000).

Agribusiness also includes a range of activities and disciplines encompassed by modern food production, and denotes the nexus between, inter alia, natural resource management, tourism and hospitality, innovation, mechanization, manufacturing, and processing activities to add value to raw materials or cash products as well as trade and distribution (Nina et al. 2010).

During the Structural Adjustment years, government encouraged backward integration but inconsistencies in macroeconomic policy initiatives between 1986 and 1995 discouraged farmers from expanding production of suitable agricultural raw materials for local processing and manufacturing. Backward integration and the privatization of state-owned enterprises are currently emphasized as a desirable policy objective by the new democratic government but growth in the manufacturing and agribusiness sector has changed very little in the past decade. Between 1990 and 1999, manufacturing including agro-industrial output in real terms actually dropped to about 92% of the level reached in 1990 (Idachaba 2000) and in contrast, the industrial sector in Nigeria (comprising manufacturing, mining, and utilities) accounts for a tiny proportion of economic activity (6%) while the manufacturing sector contributed only 4% to GDP in 2011 (Chete et al. 2013).

During the last decade, global R&D increased approximately by 22%, from $26 billion in 2000 to $31.7 billion in 2008. Arguably in context of agri-based economies, agricultural sector holds the ultimate promise to slash extreme poverty and combat chronic hunger. Increased R&D investments offer the possibilities to enhance the quantity and quality of agricultural outputs, increased income source, greater food security, and better nutrition. In the long term, investment in R&D in the agricultural sector will be crucial in all countries, in order to move the technology frontier and sustain productivity growth (Ghose 2014). And the public sector has traditionally been the driving force behind these advances and represented the lion's share of agricultural research and development (R&D) expenditures, with global public-sector R&D accounting for 55% of the US$69 billion total in 2011 (the most recent year for which global data are available) (Global Harvest Initiatives 2016).

By 2050, according to the United Nations, the world's population is estimated to reach 9.7 billion (United Nation Bulletin 2015). This presents the global agriculture sector with a daunting challenge, especially when combined with the effects of climate change and resource scarcity. The stage has been set for a potential global food crisis if policy makers and other stakeholders fail to act: Ensuring adequate supplies of food will require a 70% increase in agricultural production over the next 30 years (PricewaterhouseCoopers [PwC] 2015). The pace of agricultural innovation has increased over the last 10–15 years, with advances in genomics, software, communications, logistics, and technology. The public sector has traditionally been the driving force behind these advances and represented the lion's share of agricultural research and development (R&D) expenditures, with global public-sector R&D accounting for 55% of the US$69 billion total in 2011 (the most recent year for which global data are available) (Pardey et al. 2016a).

But more recently, constrained fiscal policies in many countries have slowed public-sector R&D growth. R&D spending in low-income countries is also lagging, particularly when measured on a per capita basis. In 2011, high-income countries spent US$17.73 per person, compared to US$1.51 in low-income countries (Pardey et al. 2016b). The imperative to raise the productivity of agricultural R&D by up to 70% over the next three decades will require the public and private sector to address several critical challenges. Speeding R&D cycles and furthering the widespread adoption of promising innovations, particularly in low-income countries are a precursor to improving outputs. The lags between successful R&D efforts and the widespread adoption of agricultural innovations tend to be long; at least 15–25 years before peak impacts, with further adoption lags that can continue for decades. Another challenge is that many of the most promising agricultural innovations are capital-intensive, and agriculture has historically been dominated by small businesses with low profitability and limited access to capital. Hence the study was aimed at analyzing the long run and short run relationship between R&D, public infrastructure and improved seed supply and to determine the response of improved seed supply to R&D and public infrastructure.

Methodology

The area of study: Nigeria is a federal republic in West Africa, bordering Benin in the west, Chad and Cameroon in the east, and Niger in the north. Its coast in the south lies on the Gulf of Guinea in the Atlantic Ocean. The country is located at 10° North of the equator and longitude 8° East of Greenwich Meridan. Nigeria is one of the largest countries in Africa, with a total geographical area of 923,768 square kilometres and an estimated population of about 138 million in 2008 (CIA 2008) with an average annual growth rate of more than 3.00% (Food and Agricultural Organization Statistics [FAOSTAT] 2005).

Methods of data collection: Secondary data consisting of annual time series covering a period of 24 years (1991–2012) was used for the study. Due to unavailability of data, maize and cassava were considered to carry out the study. Particularly, data on the values of improved Maize and Cassava seeds were obtained from Food and Agriculture Organization (FAO) of the United Nations. Data for public research and development (R&D) expenditure and public infrastructure expenditures (electricity, roads, and water supply) were obtained from World Bank development indicators data base.

Data analysis techniques: Augmented Dickey Fuller test (ADF) was used for stationary test of variables. Vector Error Correction Model (VECM) was used to analyze the effect of public infrastructure, research and development expenditure on seed supply.

Models Specification

Augmented Dickey Fuller test (ADF)

Following Oyinbo and Rekwot (2014) the Augmented Dickey Fuller (ADF) model with the constant term and trend was specified as follows:

$$\Delta Y_t = \alpha_0 + \alpha_1 t + \beta Y_{t-1} + \sum_{i=1}^{p} \delta_i \Delta Y_{t-1} + \varepsilon_t \tag{5.1}$$

where Y_t is the value of the variable of interest (improved maize and cassava seeds). α_0 is the constant, α_1 is the coefficient of the trend series, P is the lag order of the autoregressive process, Y_{t-1} is lagged value of order one of Y_{t-1} and ε_t is the error term.

Vector Error Correction Model (VECM)

$$\nabla Y_{t-i} = a_0 + \sum_{i=1}^{p} a_1 \nabla \mathrm{RD}_{t-i} + \sum_{i=1}^{p} a_2 \nabla \mathrm{ROAD}_{t-i} + \sum_{i=1}^{p} \alpha_3 \nabla \mathrm{WATER}_{t-i} + \sum_{i=1}^{p} \alpha_4 \nabla \mathrm{ELECT}_{t-i} + \mathrm{ECM}_{t-i} + \varepsilon_t \tag{5.2}$$

where

Y_t is improved maize and cassava seeds supply (Naira)
RD_t is research and development expenditure (Naira)
ROAD_t is public infrastructure expenditure on road (Naira)
WATER_t is public infrastructure expenditure on water (Naira)
ELECT_t is public infrastructure expenditure on electricity (Naira)
∇ is lag operator
a_0 is constant term (intercept)
$\alpha_1 \ldots \ldots \alpha_4$ are estimating parameters for improved seeds
ε_t = error term

Results and Discussion

The results in Table 5.1 present the summary of unit root test conducted under the ADF at level and first difference. The results indicate that all the variables under study were not stationary at level but were stationary at first difference at 1% level of significance except for maize seed, cassava seed and R&D which were stationary at both level and first difference. Therefore, by analyzing the table it shows that all the variables are stationary at first difference and are therefore characterized as I(1) process.

The result on the effect of public R&D and infrastructure expenditures on improved seeds supply was analyzed with the VECM and is presented on Table 5.2. The result showed that the coefficients of determination (R^2) for improved maize and cassava seeds were 0.81 and 0.74, respectively indicating that 81% and 74% of variation of maize and cassava seeds supply were explained, respectively by improved maize seed supply (−1), improved maize seed supply (−2); improved cassava seed supply (−1), improved cassava seed supply (−2); electricity, R&D, water, and roads expenditures. The result showed that a unit increase in improved maize supply (−1) and improved maize supply (−2) also increases improved maize seed supply by 2.99 and 1.99. It also increases improved cassava seed supply by 3.31 and 2.09. In contrast, a unit increase of improved cassava seed supply (−1) and improved cassava seed supply (−2) decreases improved maize supply by 2.8 and 1.95. It also decreases improved

Table 5.1 Unit root test (ADF TEST)

	ADF results				
	At level		*At first difference*		*Decision*
Variables	t-*statistic*	*Probability*	t-*statistic*	*Probability*	*I(1)*
MAIZE	−3.78	0.010	−5.28	0.000***	I(1)
CASSAVA	−4.42	0.002	−7.97	0.000***	I(1)
ROAD	−0.15	0.930	−3.62	0.000***	I(1)
WATER	−1.56	0.999	−6.31	0.000***	I(1)
RD	−3.63	0.052	−6.11	0.000***	I(1)
ELECT	2.18	0.990	−6.53	0.000***	I(1)

Note N.B ***Indicate stationary at 1% level of significance
Source Author's creation

Table 5.2 Effects of public R&D and infrastructure expenditures on improved seeds supply

Cointegrating Eq	*CointEq1*	
MAIZE(−1)	1.000000	
CASSAVA(−1)	−0.57 [− 4.95]	
C	−161.06	
Error correction	D(MAIZE)	D(CASSAVA)
	(1.10853)[− 3.74724]	(1.21757)[− 2.83368]
D(MAIZE(−1))	2.99***[2.83]	3.31***[2.85]
D(MAIZE(−2))	1.99***[2.70]	2.09***[2.58]
D(CASSAVA(−1))	−2.80***[− 3.13]	−3.23***[− 3.28]
D(CASSAVA(−2))	−1.95***[− 2.75]	−2.12***[− 2.71]
C	43.28[0.15]	173.38[0.57]
ELECT	−0.027[− 1.07]	−0.036[− 1.37]
ROAD	0.018*[1.84]	0.019*[1.80]
WATER	0.003[0.66]	0.005[0.98]
RD	0.38**[2.07]	0.27***[3.49]
R-squared	0.817410	0.747948
Adj. *R*-squared	0.634820	0.495896
Sum sq. resids	88824.87	107159.2
S.E. equation	99.34501	109.1173
F-statistic	4.476749	2.967436
Log likelihood	−107.2347	−109.0173
Akaike AIC	12.34049	12.52814
Schwarz SC	12.83756	13.02521
Mean dependent	0.852632	−0.094737
S.D. dependent	164.3965	153.6857
Determinant resid covariance (dof adj.)		13974551
Determinant resid covariance		3135564.
Log likelihood		−196.0237
Akaike information criterion		22.94986
Schwarz criterion		24.04342

Note N.B ***, ** and * are significant at 1, 5 and 10%, respectively; NB values in bracket are *t* values. Several studies confirm *t* agricultural expenditure on R&D is an important driver of productivity growth
Source Author's creation

cassava supply by 3.23 and 2.12. Also a unit increase in government expenditures on roads increased improved maize and cassava seeds supply by 0.018 and 0.019, respectively and this could be attributed to the fact that road is among basic infrastructure for sustainable agricultural development. This finding conforms with the study of Lokesha and

Mahesha (2016) that Rural roads are the wealth of a nation, a tool for social inclusion, economic development and environmental sustainability thereby reducing transport cost and stimulating marketing. Similarly; a unit increase in R&D expenditure increases improved maize and cassava seeds supply by 0.38 and 0.27, respectively and this could also be due to the fact that research provides innovation in the agricultural sector. This finding is in line with the study of Alene (2010), which states that agricultural expenditure on R&D is an important driver of productivity growth.

The result of the response of improved seeds supply to increase R&D expenditure and decrease in public infrastructure expenditure by 5% is presented in Table 5.3. The result indicated that the simulated scenario 1 for improved cassava seed supply ranges between 101.12 and 201.13 with a mean value of 160.29 Naira compared to the baseline which ranges between 99.16 and 197.87 with mean of 156.71. As for improved maize seed supply; the result indicated that the simulated scenario 1 ranges between 103.15 and 515.59 with the mean value of 349.59 Naira compared to the baseline, which ranges between 111.66 and 482.95 with a mean value of 332.23 Naira. These results imply that increase in government spending's on R&D and decrease in public infrastructure expenditure will increase the quantity of improved cassava and maize seeds supply thereby increasing agricultural productivity (Figs. 5.1 and 5.2).

The result of the response of improved maize and cassava seeds supply to increases in R&D and public infrastructure expenditures by 5% is presented in Table 5.4. The result indicated that the simulated scenario 2 for improved maize seed supply ranges between 124.05 and 522.35

Table 5.3 Summary statistics for response of improved seed supply to increase in R&D and decrease in public infrastructure by 5%

	Improved cassava seed supply		*Improved maize seed supply*	
	Baseline	*Scenario 1*	*Baseline*	*Scenario 1*
Mean	156.71	160.29	332.23	349.59
Minimum	99.16	101.12	111.66	103.15
Maximum	197.87	201.13	482.95	515.59
Std deviation	26.31	26.86	103.41	117.87

Source Author's creation

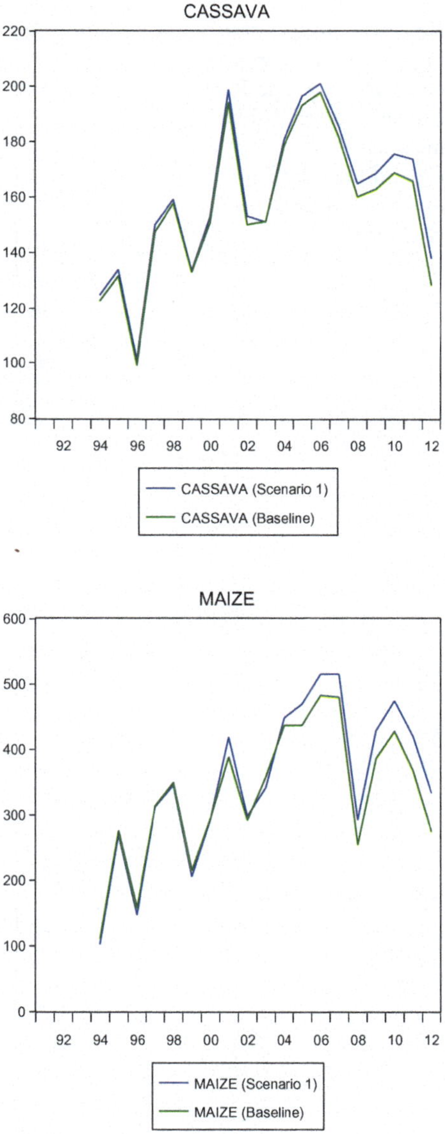

Fig. 5.1 Response of improved seed supply to increase in public R&D and decrease in public infrastructure expenditures by 5% (*Source* Author's creation)

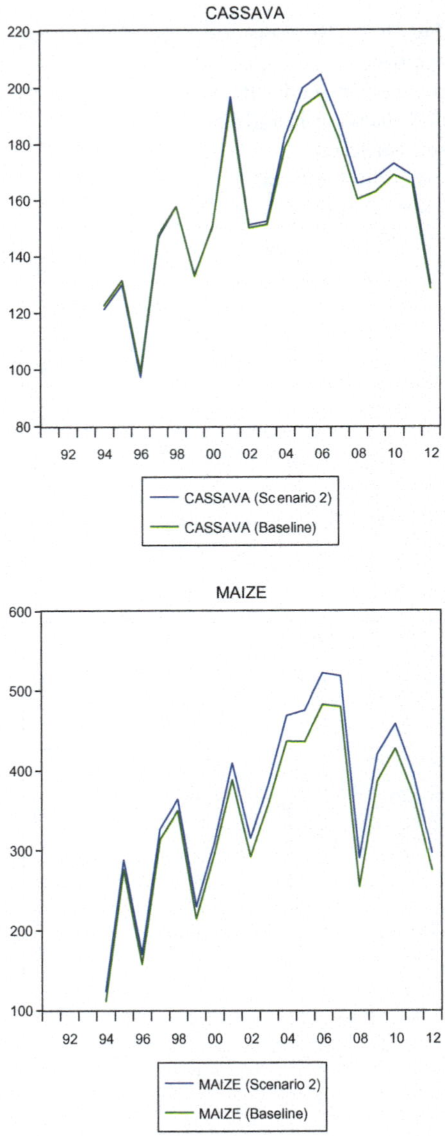

Fig. 5.2 Response of improved seed supply to increases in public R&D and increase in public infrastructure expenditures by 5% (*Source* Author's creation)

Table 5.4 Summary statistics for response of improved seed supply to increase in R&D and increase in public infrastructure by 5%

	Improved maize seed supply		*Improved cassava seed supply*	
	Baseline	*Scenario 2*	*Baseline*	*Scenario 2*
Mean	332.32	356.40	156.71	158.93
Minimum	111.66	124.05	99.16	97.43
Maximum	482.95	522.35	197.87	204.67
Std deviation	103.41	111.14	26.31	28.74

Source Author's creation

with a mean value of 356.40 Naira compared to the baseline which ranges between 111.66 and 482.95 with mean of 332.32 Naira. As for improved cassava seeds supply, the result indicated that the simulated scenario 2 ranges between 97.43 and 204.67 with a mean value of 158.93 Naira compared to baseline which ranges between 99.16 and 197.87 with a mean value of 156.71. This result implies that increase in government spending's on R&D and infrastructure will increase the quantity of seeds supply, thereby increasing agricultural productivity.

Conclusion

The study analyzed the response of improved seeds (maize and cassava) supply to public infrastructure, research and development expenditure in Nigeria and it was found that increased government spending in both infrastructure and R&D promoted the supply of improved seed during the period under review. Based on the findings, it was concluded that increased government spending in infrastructure and R&D are paramount for the sustainability of agricultural business in Nigeria.

It is therefore recommended that government should increase budget allocation for research and development. It is also recommended that government should invest in renewable energy to ensure steady power supply. Furthermore; it is recommended that government should improve on its budget allocation on road construction and focus on irrigation farming as two of the Nigeria irrigation schemes, Kampe-Omi and Tada-Shonga, under Lower Niger River Basin Development Authority, received less than 50% of the funds required for their operations between 2004 and 2018.

References

AGRA. (2013). *The Africa Agriculture Status Report: Focus on Staple Crops*. Alliance for a Green Revolution in Africa, Nairobi. http://agra-alliance.org/our-results/agra-status-reports.

Alene, A. D. (2010). Productivity Growth and Effects of R&D in African Agriculture. *Agricultural Economics, 41*, 223–238.

Chete, L. N., Adeoti, J. O., Adeyinka, F. M., & Ogundele, O. (2013). *Industrial Development and Growth in Nigeria: Lessons and Challenge*. Learning to Compete (Working Paper 8, 40 pp.).

CIA. (2008). *CIA—World Factbook*. http://www.cia.gov/library/publications/the-worldfactbook/print/ni.html.

Food and Agricultural Organization Statistics Division (FAOSTAT). (2005). *Average Annual Growth Rates of Food and Population of Nigeria, 1990–2003*.

FANRPAN. (2010). *FANRPAN Launches Regional Seed Project to Boost Food Security*. Food Agriculture and Natural Resources Policy Analysis Network, Pretoria. http://www.fanrpan.org/documents/d00858/SA_SSP_press_release.pdf.

Ghose, B. (2014). Promoting Agricultural Research and Development to Strengthen Food Security in South Asia. *International Journal of Agronomy, 4*, 6.

Gill, R., Bates, A., Bicksler, R., Burnette, V., & Ricciardi, L. Y. (2013). Strengthening Informal Seed Systems to Enhance Food Security in Southeast. *Journal of Agriculture Food Systems and Community Development, 3*, 139–153.

Global Harvest Initiative. (2016). *2016 Global Agricultural Productivity Report® (GAP Report®)*. Washington, DC: Global Harvest Initiative. Available at http://www.globalharvestinitiative.org/index.php/gapreport-gap-index/2016-gap-report.

Gyawali, S. (2010). Participatory Crop Improvement and Formal Release of Jethobudho Rice Landrace in Nepali. *Euphytica, 176*, 59–78.

Idachaba F. S. (2000). *Agricultural Policy Process in Africa: Role of Policy Analysts*. ECAPAPA Monograph Series 2, Eastern and Central Africa Programme for Agricultural Policy Analysis, A Program of the Association for Strengthening Agricultural Research in Eastern and Central Africa (ASARECA), Entebbe Uganda.

Kugbei, S., Turner, M., & Witthaut, P. (Eds.). (2000). *Finance and Management of Small-Scale Seed Enterprises*. ICARDA, Aleppo, Syria.

Lacoste, M., Williams, R., Erskine, W., Nesbitt, H., Pereira, L., & Marçal, A. (2012). Varietal Diffusion in Marginal Seed Systems: Participatory Trials Initiate Change in East Timor. *Journal of Crop Improvement, 26*(2012), 468–488.

Lokesha, M. N., & Mahesha, M. (2016). Impact of Road Infrastructure on Agricultural Development Programme in India. *International Journal of Humanities and Social Science Invention, 5*(11), 1–7.

Nina, F., Matthias, H., & Theuvsen, L. (2010). Sustainability Management in Agribusiness: Challenges, Concepts, Responsibilities and Performance; Trans Forum's Approach. *Agronomy for Sustainable Development, 6*(8), 12–20.

Oyinbo, O., & Rekwot, G. Z. (2014). The Relationships of Inflationary Trend, Agricultural Productivity and Economic Growth in Nigeria. *CBN Journal of Applied Statistics, 5*(1), 35–47.

Pardey, P. G., Chan-Kang, C., Dehmer, S., & Beddow, J. M. (2016a, April). *Shifting Ground: Food and Agriculture R&D Spending Worldwide, 1960–2011.* St. Paul: International Science and Technology Practice and Policy center, University of Minnesota.

Pardey, P. G., Chan-Kang, C., Dehmer, S., & Beddow, J. M. (2016b, September 15). Agricultural R&D Is on the Move. *Nature, 537*, 301–303 (and online supplement at go.nature.com/2cfvkij).

Pawa, T. (2013). Agribusiness as a Veritable Tool for Rural Development in Nigeria. *International Letters of Social and Humanistic Sciences Online, 14,* 26–36.

PricewaterhouseCoopers (PwC). (2015). Annual Report.

Rajalahti, R. (2013, May 2). *The World Bank Support to Seed Sector Development.* In Supporting Comprehensive Seed Sector Development. Washington, DC.

Tin, H. Q., Cuc, N. H., Be, T. T., Ignacio, N., & Berg, T. (2011). Impacts of Seed Clubs in Ensuring Local Seed Systems in the Mekong Delta. *Vietnam Journal Sustainable. Agriculture, 35*(2011), 840–854.

United Nation Bulletin. (2015). https://www.un.org/development/desa/en/news/population/2015-report.html. Accessed in December, 2019.

See http://www.un.org/en/development/desa/news/population/2015-report.html for more on population growth estimates.

CHAPTER 6

Understanding the Nutrition, Health, Climate Change, Deforestation, and Land Access Nexus

Gbadebo Odularu, Mariama Deen-Swarray, and Bamidele Adekunle

The Nexus Picture

Eating a rich diet that comprises a colorful variety of fruits and vegetables helps people stay healthy and prevents many chronic diseases and conditions such as cancers, bone density, cardiovascular diseases, obesity, etc.

This is not needed here for the summary of the article. This can be streamlined as the focus is on the article itself and its critique (the summary even should be far less involved than the critique).

G. Odularu (✉)
Department of Economics and Finance, Bay Atlantic University, Washington, DC, USA

M. Deen-Swarray
Research Associate, Research ICT Africa (RIA), Cape Town, South Africa

Research Manager, BBC Media Action, Freetown, Sierra Leone

G. Odularu (ed.), *Nutrition, Sustainable Agriculture and Climate Change in Africa*,
https://doi.org/10.1007/978-3-030-47875-9_6

(Mason-D'Croz et al. 2019; Alissa and Ferns 2017). However, over the last couple of decades, and in spite of the nutrition assistance advocacy programs being implemented by the Government, there exists huge gap between current fruit and vegetable intake, and those recommended in the 2015–2020 Dietary Guidelines for Americans (DGAs)[1] (HHS 2015). Invariably, many Americans continually chose high-fat, high-calorie foods largely due to unprecedented increase in the production and sale of cheap calories, highly processed, fast foods, and overconsumption.

According to the Centers for Disease Control and Prevention (CDC) State Indicator Report on Fruits and Vegetables, 2018,[2] only 1 in 10 US adults consume 1.5–2 cups of fruits and 2–3 cups of vegetables per day, just 9% and 2% of high school students, respectively, meet the fruits and vegetables recommendation, while FV consumption is quite low among American youth (CDC 2018; Moore et al. 2017; HHS 2015). Further, this CDC Report discusses the increasing levels of income-related disparities, such that 7% of adults who live at or below the poverty level are compared to 11.4% of adults with the highest household incomes in meeting the daily vegetable recommendation (CDC 2018; Moore et al. 2017) interest in healthy, plant-based foods creates opportunities for fruits and vegetables in snack and bakery products. The 2015–2020 Dietary Guidelines recommends consuming 2 cups equivalents of fruits and 2.5 cup equivalents of vegetables per day, based on a 2000-calorie diet. However, according to a 2017 CDC study, just 1 out of 10 adults meet the recommended levels. By implications, adults are missing out on essential nutrients inherently found in fruits and vegetables (vegetables provide nutrients like dietary fiber, potassium, vitamins A, vitamins C, copper, magnesium, vitamin E, vitamin B6, folate, iron, manganese, thiamine, and niacin; Fruits are high in fiber, vitamins, minerals such as vitamin C, potassium and folate and antioxidants).

[1] The 2015–2020 *Dietary Guidelines for Americans* recommends that adults consume 1.5–2 cups of fruits and 2–3 cups of vegetables per day.

[2] The CDC State Indicator Report on Fruits and Vegetables, 2018, shows the status of 10 indicators of fruits and vegetables access and production by state.

B. Adekunle
School of Environmental Design and Rural Development,
University of Guelph, Guelph, ON, Canada

According to the African Development Bank (AfDB)'s projections, Africa's net food imports (rice, sugar, soybeans, maize, oil, beef, potatoes, etc.) could amount to about US$110 billion by 2025, while the number of undernourished people would rise from 240 million in 2015 to about 320 million in 2025. While Pre-COVID-19 outbreak food security situation shows that 135 million people were experiencing severe hunger such that it threatened their lives and livelihood, the current and rapidly evolving COVID-19 has doubled this scenario such that a globally estimated 9 million people will die of hunger annually (mainly children in poorer countries) (World Food Programme 2020).

At the community, national, regional, and global levels, food and nutrition (in)security (FNI) contribute to public health problems for individuals as well as posing considerable macroeconomic burden on countries. In 2018, an estimated 1 in 9 Americans were food insecure, equating to over 37 million Americans, including more than 11 million children (Hunger and Health 2017). Effective responses to FNI must address the overlapping challenges posed by the social determinants of health (USDA 2019; Healthy People 2020). According to Bacon and Baker (2017), food banks served an estimated of 46 million people in the U.S in 2015. Although the vast majority of food and nutrition insecure people live in the developing world, the study further shows that increasing number of individuals continue to rely on private food assistance in the US, the United Kingdom, Australia, Canada, and other high-income countries. In order to foster global nutrition security and global health, especially in other developing countries in the global south, the World Food Program (WFP), works with governments and partners to help vulnerable groups, such as women, children, and people receiving treatment for HIV and tuberculosis, access nutritious diets (WFP 2019). Some of the WFP programs which are aimed at promoting global nutrition and health include distributing Specialized Nutritious Foods, fortifying staples, designing and implementing school feeding and enabling dietary diversification. Food and nutrition insecurity (FNI) do not exist in isolation in the sense that low-income families are affected by multiple challenges such as social isolation, low wages, high medical costs, housing shortage, chronic health problems, and illiteracy. Taken together, these challenges and similar ones are important social determinants of health. Thus, effective responses to FNI must address the overlapping challenges posed by the social determinants of health (USDA 2019; Healthy People 2020).

According to FAO (2010), CSA involves agriculture that sustainably increases productivity and resilience (adaptation), reduces/removes GHGs (mitigation), and enhances achievement of national food security and development goals. From the perspective of the Africa CSA Alliance, CSA offers triple wins, which include: significant potential to enhance food and nutrition security for all people at all times, taking account of the need for adaptation in response to current and near-term effects of climate change and, where in the interests of smallholder farmers, mitigation to reduce the future threats to global food security. A bulk of the academic and policy literature has focused primarily on the effects of climate change on agricultural productivity.[2] In other words, a few studies have been conducted to date specifically focusing on climate change and understanding its impact pathway in addressing mal- and undernutrition challenges in Africa. In most analysis, socioeconomic impacts hit agricultural sectors disproportionately hard, as many conflicts are fought in rural areas and targeting agricultural assets such as land. Domestic and foreign private investments in land are some of the root causes of violence, and the conflict over land increased competition for land, thereby affecting women's access and communal nutrition outcomes. Though conflicts over land result in undernutrition, few studies have also documented a reverse causal link in which socioeconomic and political grievances trigger conflict. Though emphasizing food security at the expense of food sovereignty and food self-sufficiency, the Principles for Responsible Agricultural Investment (RAI) anticipate that investment agreements could include "call options," which can prevent exit of unacceptably large food volumes from the country when specific market conditions occur (Schutter 2011). Further, the literature is replete with accounts of the adverse impacts of deforestation on the economic growth in Africa. For instance, Sierra Leone faces several challenges as it embarks on the process of ensuring economic growth following years of civil unrest. Extraction, deforestation, and land degradation are on the increase and in some instances, this has been attributed to the lack of effective policies and the inability to enforce those in existence. The rate of deforestation has increased by 7.3% since the end of the civil war and years of engaging in these activities has reduced the country's forest cover by over 70%. With

[2] These studies have focused on the relationship between farm size and productivity, sharecropping tenancy distortions, access to credit, investment incentives, and labor supply resulting from security of property rights.

these statistics and the various development processes going on in the country, it is of utmost importance to understand the factors that influence the rate of deforestation and provide informed advice that will assist policy makers to avert the imminent socioeconomic and environmental catastrophe.

Property rights over land shape investments, labor supply, long-term policy outcomes, environment, and violence (Fenske 2014). There has been increasing evidence of widespread land acquisition for agro-fuels production in collaboration with governments in a broad selection of Sub-Saharan African countries. Deininger (2011) noted that between January 2008 and April 2010, about four million hectares of average annual global agricultural lands were expanded. Friis and Reenberg (2010) found the evidence that land deals (sale or long-term leases totaling between 51 and 63 million hectares, roughly the size of France) had been finalized or were in negotiation in Sub-Saharan Africa alone. Though, land investors are mainly governments of food insecure countries in the Middle East and Asia which invest in food production beyond their borders, it must, however, be repeatedly stressed that EU companies which are interested in agro-fuel production make up a significant proportion of these investments, with 31 agro-fuels related land deals in 2009–2010 in Madagascar and Ethiopia alone (ibid.). Indeed, in 2012, the International Land Coalition reported that three quarters of land deals in developing countries between 2000 and 2012 were for biofuels production (Anseeuw et al. 2012). Though emphasizing food security at the expense of food sovereignty and food self-sufficiency, the Principles for Responsible Agricultural Investment (RAI) anticipate that investment agreements could include "call options," "which can prevent exit of unacceptably large food volumes from the country when specific market conditions occur" (Schutter 2011).

In view of the threats that land inequality poses to the rural poor, land issues scholars have proposed reform of land governance frameworks as one of the most effective solutions. In other words, integration of customary land governance with formal legal land frameworks may hold the key to land negotiations that protect land rights and promote commercial investment (FAO 2010). Further, contrasting government policies to address wide disparities in land access range from legislation to protect and expand protection of land rights to radical land distribution to smallholder farmers as well as moderate measures to protect land rights for marginal groups. In addition, formulating effective and successful decentralization of land institutions to district and local levels or establishing program network between land management and poverty reduction initiatives will facilitate a process of strengthening the sustainability of land interventions (ILC 2009).

The impact of large-scale land acquisitions (land grabbing) by foreign investors on food and nutrition security is quite controversial. Foreign investors are interested in outsourcing food production, or in replacing food crops by cash crops (e.g., energy crops)—thus worsening food and nutrition security in the host society (IFPRI 2011), Deninger and Byerlee (2011), and Schutter (2011), and this will likely jeopardize host country food nutrition outlook. There are other arguments not in favor of large-scale land acquisitions such as marginalization and eviction of small farmer holders (communal land users), race to the bottom due to the competition between poor countries in order to attract foreign investors, weak governance, corruption, and elite capture.

An index of Women's Empowerment in Agriculture' (WEAI).[3] combining five domains of empowerment and sub-index and a gender-parity index, showed a significant and positive association with calorie availability, household dietary diversity, and nutrition outcomes for women and children, depending on the dimension of empowerment (Galiani and Schargrodsky 2004; Allendorf 2007; Vogl 2007; Malapit et al. 2013; Menon et al. 2014; Owusu et al. 2016; Dumas et al. 2018).

Land is one of the three major factors of production as stipulated in classical economics and therefore very important in economies that rely heavily on agriculture. Effecting changes in the use of land is thus necessary for economic and social development. Converting any particular piece of land for another purpose can however have its costs (Wu 2008). This cost is to a large extent environmental and though economic and social costs are factored into land use decisions, the externalities from environmental related issues are not.

According to the Food and Agriculture Organization, the annual rates of deforestation in the developing world were estimated at 15.5 million hectares between 1980 and 1990 and a little lower at 13.7 million hectares between 1990 and 1995. According to these statistics, about 200 million hectares of total forest area were lost during the entire period.

[3] Women's autonomy in agricultural production decisions remains one of the impactfully positive effects on enhancing maternal and child nutrition outcomes, in terms of both BMIs, HAZ, WHZ and WAZ scores.

In Africa in particular, the practice of deforestation has been adopted as a result of many issues. Countries engage in this practice as they strive to achieve economic development and improve the well-being of their citizens. Interestingly though, the majority of deforested areas have been found to be unsuitable for long-term farming and grazing activities, causing them to rapidly lose their value once the forests have been cut and burnt (Fiset 2010).

Deforestation can be as a result of direct and indirect factors. The direct causes identified include mainly, the promotion of commercial agriculture, livestock grazing, mining, and petroleum exploration. Key among the indirect factors are fiscal policies, agriculture policies, forestry policy and management, land tenure, access and pressures from the market as demand for forest products rise.

Many governments, faced with political decisions on sustainable food production, employment creation, structural adjustments in the economy and increasing urban migration, have not given enough focus to deforestation. In most cases, they deliberately allow deforestation to continue, using it as a social and economic haven (Tripathy 2011). It has been cited that the major causes of deforestation are often a reflection of the political and economic distortions in an economy (Godoy et al. 1996). Some scholars have attributed the increase in environmental degradation and deforestation to economic development (Painter and Durham, 1995).

Forest areas and the trees often found in them are very important and play a vital role in the environment and in the lives of humans as well as animals. They are essentially major contributors to activities on our planet. Our forest and trees are however being depleted at alarmingly high rates. Achieving short-term economic benefits has been at the center as to why countries engage in deforestation. Forests are often cleared for construction purposes as urbanization increases and the need for more land area increases and trees become a source of fuel for many. Another major reason often cited for deforestation is the need to expand agricultural activities. All these are carried out with little or no regard for the environmental impact, the health hazards, the social implications, and ultimately the long-run economic effects. Embarking on infrastructure development also tends to lead governments to resort to deforestation and this has also been the case in Sierra Leone.

Thus, environmental policy reform efforts explicitly emphasize the need for countries to carefully balance productive and redistributive goals. As a corollary, in order to manage the challenges of natural resources (forest, land, etc.) led growth path successfully, developing countries, need to design and implement comprehensive, inclusive and rights-based socioeconomic policies; build strong democratic institutions; and be given the policy space to foster productive diversification while safeguarding macroeconomic stability (UNRISD 2012) increase in environmental degradation and deforestation to economic development (Painter and Dure 1995).

A Glance at Theory and Literature

The Modernization theory argues that a relationship exists between nutritional outcomes and sustainable development on one hand, and deforestation and environmental degradation on the other hand. It also shows that deforestation increases when development is at its early stages, levels off and finally declines as the economy reaches its peak growth. Those of the World-Systems theory contradicts this view, arguing that deforestation increases as a result of unbalanced economic relations whereby the environmental impact of developed nations is transferred to poorer and less developed nations. The Neo-Malthusian theory brings the focus to demographic related factors, stressing that they are key contributing factors to the rate of deforestation.

The poverty-environment scenario is one of the arguments put forward to explain the reasons for activities that lead to deforestation. This theory establishes a link between deforestation and poverty. The belief is that in order to establish a source of livelihood, the poor in society engage in deforestation activities. Contrary to this argument is the one, which maintains that the poor have no reason to engage in deforestation, as they lack the required capital to increase production.

Models, which assume that the main aim of farmers is to maximize profit, argue that higher prices of agricultural products are expected to increase the rate of deforestation. Monela (1995) supports this assumption, showing that higher prices increase deforestation. Some models on the other hand, use the preference for subsistence-type farming to explain the decision of farmers to engage in deforestation. These models maintain that once farmers have satisfied their minimum consumption level, they will choose leisure over more land for production. In such instances, increased demand for agricultural products will not have an increasing effect on the rate of deforestation. The rationale behind this is that with higher prices, farmers are able to make enough to meet their basic consumption needs without having to increase production. Angelsen (1999) assuming this subsistence behavior reveals that deforestation decreases when agricultural prices rise.

Conclusion, Proposed Model, and Policy Suggestions

One of the strategic goals of the United Nations Sustainable Development Goal 2 (UN SDG 2) is to eliminate hunger and foster nutrition security, as a vital component of healthy social, cognitive, and physical development in children, older adults, and other minorities. Every day, Africans become poor and food insecure, forcing them to make difficult food choices and struggling with hunger as an epidemic amid the COVID-19 pandemic. By educating ourselves about these issues, we can collaborate to eliminate hunger boldly and confidently in our communities. There is an increasing role for non-governmental and community development organizations toward awareness creation as well as offering coordinated support to community residents. This support should provide food to residents who are in need. However, these NGOs' services delivery impact could be enhanced with the selected nutrition and sustainable agriculture policy interventions are implemented. The nutrition and sustainable agriculture research intervention or model which is being proposed in this paper is a community food and nutrition needs assessment and sustainable agriculture (CFNNASA) intervention, which will influence how CSA, nutrition and agri-food outcomes are evolving and the challenges inherent in measuring nutrition outcomes from a broad food distribution, environmental awareness, and health services research perspectives.

Within this proposed model, the nutrition and sustainable agri-food policy research center will investigate questions like measuring what happens to the food once it reaches the household? Is the food consumed? And by whom? by embarking on longitudinal health profile of patients that have utilized food distribution programs toward bolstering the rationale for the collaborative initiative. The proposed research center will also advocate for evidence-based policies that encourage healthier eating, and improved health.

A proposed model starts with the initial contact between NGO, research center, and a health center. As NGO uses its food insecurity and meal distribution maps to identify selected residents, a health center will reach out to the NGO after identifying a food and nutrition issue through the CFNNA. The research center will develop a proposal for submission to the national or regional government for funding to validate and co-implement the model. Thus, in collaboration with research center, community health center will offer three-pronged approach to addressing FNI: mobile market, screening, and a tool kit. After implementing the model for a year or two, the research center will use randomized controlled trials to test its impact on the nutritional outcomes of specific low-income population will inform whether effective food distribution directly affect outcomes. Most importantly, it will increase accessibility of locally produced fresh fruits and vegetables, increase consumption of locally produced fresh fruits and vegetables among low-income residents, and implement a standardized system for scaling, implementing, and evaluating the impact of its program. It will aim to foster and sustain healthy dietary behaviors, especially among low-income residents.

While leveraging on selected food assistance programs which provide access to fresh, local produce at a variety of retail outlets, this proposed model will also ensure that everyone has access to affordable, nutritious food and information to make healthy decisions, especially among patients at risk for diet-related diseases and food insecurity. Engaging doctors and other health professionals to provide prescriptions for their patients that are redeemable at participating supermarkets, corner stores and farmers or mobile markets for fresh produce.

Lack or inadequacy of access to nutritious, affordable foods, coupled with a lack of education on how to make healthy choices, are major contributors to obesity, diabetes, and other diet-related diseases. As a result, many healthcare providers now use modern tools to screen for food insecurity and are eager to offer resources to patients and their families. It will be implemented and evaluated in partnership with healthcare providers, with the purpose of tracking health outcomes, changes in healthcare usage and costs, and changes in produce consumption.

A research center could assess how well the food insecure population is being served by food banks, NGOs, and other food distribution agencies. This is because accessibility remains a major challenge to many clients, especially when food assistance remains inaccessible due to location, transportation options, hours of operation, timeliness, knowledge to know where to go and when, and other barriers (disability, age, illness, children, social stigma, etc.) within a complex and constantly changing landscape of provides and other resources. Thus, since the NGO may have limited relationship capacity with the community and the population that it serves, and also lack direct control over the distribution of food, research center could adopt a geographic information systems (GIS) to assess how well food and nutrition assistance programs are addressing proximity dimensions of access in serving food insecure populations in the community. Thereafter, leveraging on this to understand how global food assistance programs are effective in delivering food to low-income countries in the world.

One of the likely reasons behind the nutrition-related institutional challenges is that most policy interventions tend to focus on agricultural production metrics, with limited focus on enhancing the quality of research toward improving nutrition outcomes on the continent. In order for Africa to realize the national food and nutrition security goals (as well as the United Nations Sustainable Development Goals (UN SDGs 2 & 4), there must be a policy and paradigm shift from political rhetoric to actual malnutrition metrics focusing on targeted access to healthy food, quality of food in terms of proteins, micronutrients, and vitamins, access to clean water, evidence-based commitments to food and nutrition security, systematic assessment of progress toward achieving nutrition security and adequate investments in improved nutrition programs aimed at targeting the Africa.

Increased awareness creation, knowledge dissemination, and capacity strengthening on Enhanced Implementation of Sustainable Agriculture Strategies and Programmes are required to mitigate a looming COVID-19 triggered hunger pandemic and shocks. The short to medium- and long-term impacts of COVID-19 pandemic on the national, regional and global agri-food, trade, aviation, maritime, logistics, and other socioeconomic sectors cannot be overemphasized.

Enhancing nutrition and sustainable agriculture outcomes is much more than production of environmental management and quality food in adequate quantity but the adoption and implementation of agricultural policies were being nutrition sensitive as well as multi sector in approach.

References

Africa Growth Initiative (AGI). (2017). *Ending Rural Hunger: The Cases of Ethiopia, Ghana, Nigeria, Senegal, Uganda and Tanzania*. The Brookings Institute Global Development Project on 'Ending Rural Hunger'. www.endingruralhunger.org.

Alissa, E. M., & Ferns, G. A. (2017). Dietary Fruits and Vegetables and Cardiovascular Diseases Risk. *Critical Review in Food Science Nutrition, 57*, 1950–1962.

Allendorf, K. (2007). Do Women's Land Rights Promote Empowerment and Child Health in Nepal? *World Development, 35*(11), 1975–1988.

Angelsen, A. (1999). Agricultural Expansion and Deforestation: Modeling the Impact of Population, Market Forces and Property Rights. *Journal of Development Economics, 58*, 185–218.

Anseeuw, W., Alden Wily, L., Cotula, L., & Taylor, M. (2012). *Land Rights and the Rush for Land. Findings of the Global Commercial Pressures on Land Research Project*. Rome: ILC.

Bacon, C. M., & Baker, G. A. (2017). *Agriculture and Human Values, 34*, 899. https://doi.org/10.1007/s10460-017-9783-y.

Centers for Disease Control and Prevention (CDC). (2018). *State Indicator Report on Fruits and Vegetables*. Atlanta, GA: U.S. Department of Health and Human Services.

Deninger, K. W., & Byerlee, D. (2011). *Rising Global Interest in Farmland: Can it Yield Sustainable and Equitable Benefits?* The World Bank.

Dumas, S. E., Kassa, L., Young, S. L., & Travis, A. J. (2018). Examining the Association Between Livestock Ownership Typologies and Child Nutrition in the Luangwa Valley, Zambia. *PLoS ONE, 13*(2), e0191339. https://doi.org/10.1371/journal.pone.0191339.

FAO. (2010). *Africa's Changing Landscape: Securing Land Access for the Rural Poor*. Accra, Ghana: FAO Regional Office for Africa.

Fenske, J. (2014, September). Trees, Tenure and Conflict: Rubber in Colonia Benin. *Journal of Development Economics, 110*, 226–238.

Fiset, N. (2010). The Positive and Negative Consequences of Deforestation. *More Tree Articles*, September 25, 2010.

Friis, C., & Reenberg, A. (2010). *Land Grab in Africa: Emerging Land System Drivers in a Teleconnected World* (GLP Report No. 1). Copenhagen: GLP-IPO.

Galiani, S., & Schargrodsky, E. (2004). Effects of Land Titling on Child Health. *Economics & Human Biology, 2*(3), 353–372.

Godoy, R., Franks, J. R., & Alvarado, M. (1996). *Adoption of Modern Agricultural Technologies by Lowland Amerindians in Bolivia: The Role of Households, Villages, Ethnicity and Markets*. Cambridge, MA: Havard Institute for International Development.

Healthy People. (2020). *Social Determinants of Health*. Available online at https://www.healthypeople.gov/2020/topics-objectives/topic/social-determinants-of-health.

IFPRI. (2011). *Foreign Direct Investment in Land in West Africa*.

ILC. (2009). *Increasing Commercial Pressure on Land: Building a Coordinated Response*. www.landcoalition.org.

Malapit, H. J. L., Kadiyala, S., Quisumbing, A. R., Cunningham, K., & Tyagi, P. (2013). *Women's Empowerment in Agriculture, Production Diversity and Nutrition* (IFPRI Discussion Paper 01313).

Mason-D'Croz, D., Bogard, J., Sulser, T., Cenacchi, N., Dunston, S., Herrero, M., & Wiebe, K. (2019). Gaps between fruit and vegetable production, demand, and recommended consumption at global and national levels: an integrated modelling study. *The Lancet Planetary Health, 3*(7), e318–e329.

Menon, N., van der Meulen Rodgers, Y., & Nguyen, H. (2014). Women's Land Rights and Children's Human Capital in Vietnam. *World Development, 54*, 18–31. https://doi.org/10.1016/j.worlddev.2013.07.005.

Monela, G. C. (1995). *Tropical Rainforest Deforestation, Biodiversity Benefits and Sustainable Land Use: An Analysis of Economic and Ecological Aspects Related to the Nguru Mountains, Tanzania*. PhD. Dissertation. Agricultural University of Norway, Department of Forest Sciences, Aas.

Moore, L. V., Thompson, F. E., & Demissie, Z. (2017). Percentage of Youth Meeting Federal Fruit and Vegetable Intake Recommendations: Youth Risk Behavior Surveillance System, United States and 33 States, 2013. *Journal of the Academy of Nutrition and Dietetics, 117*(4), 545–553.

Nutrition/World Food Program. (2019). Retrieved from wfp.org website. https://www.wfp.org/nutrition.

Owusu, J. S., Colecraft, E. K., Aryeetey, R., Vaccaro, J. A., & Huffman, F. G. (2016). Nutrition Intakes and Nutritional Status of School Age Children in Ghana. *Journal of Food Research*. Canadian Center of Science and Education. Available from: https://www.researchgate.net/publication/313411333_Nutrition_Intakes_and_Nutritional_Status_of_School_Age_Children_in_Ghana. Accessed October 14, 2018 and October 5, 2019.

Painter, M., & Durham, W. (1995). *The Social Causes of Environment Degradation in Latin America*. Ann Arbor MI, USA: University of Michigan Press.

Schutter, O. D. (2011). How Not to Think of Land-Grabbing: Three Critiques of Large-Scale Investments in Farmland. *The Journal of Peasant Studies, 38*(2), 249–279. https://doi.org/10.1080/03066150.2011.559008.

Tripathy, R. K. (2011). *1103 words article on Deforestation*. http://www.preservearticles.com/201103314843/article-on-deforestation.html.

UNRISD Research and Policy Brief 16. (2012). *Mineral Rents and the Financing of Social Policy: Options and Constraints*. United Nations Research Institute for Social Development, December 2012.

US Department of Agriculture. (2019). *Definitions of Food Security*. Available online at https://www.ers.usda.gov/topics/food-nutrition-assistance/food-security-in-the-us/definitions-of-food-security.aspx.

US Department of Health and Human Services (HHS) & US Department of Agriculture (USDA). (2015). *The 2015–2020 Dietary Guidelines for Americans*. 8th Edition. December 2015. Available at: http://health.gov/dietaryguidelines/2015/guidelines/.

Vogl, T. S. (2007). Urban Land Rights and Child Nutritional Status in Peru, 2004. *Economics & Human Biology, 5*(2), 302–321. https://doi.org/10.1016/j.ehb.2007.01.001.

What Is Food Insecurity in America? Hunger and Health. (2017). Retrieved from Hunger and Health website. https://hungerandhealth.feedingamerica.org/understand-food-insecurity/.

World Food Program (WFP). (2020). *Risk of Hunger Pandemic as COVID-19 Set to Almost Double Acute Hunger by End of 2020*, viewed 5 May 2020. https://insight.wfp.org/cOVID-19-willalmost-double-people-in-acute-hunger-by-end-of-2020-59df0c4a8072.

Wu, J. (2008). Land Use Changes: Economic, Social, and Environmental Impacts. *The Magazine of Food, Farm and Resource Issues,* 4th Quarter 2008, *23*(4).

CHAPTER 7

Gender, Rural Communities and Sustainable Development in South Africa

Olufunmilayo Odularu and Priscilla Monyai

Introduction: Understanding Sustainable Development

Sustainable livelihood includes the capabilities, assets and activities required for a means of living. Potential likelihood helps to generate more income, improved food security reduced vulnerability and improved well-being. Others are the free hand it gives developmental practitioners, and more process-oriented development activities. Development discourse is dominated by two approaches to the understanding of sustainable livelihoods. The first approach takes an economic view based on employment, production, as well as household income. The second is more holistic in nature as it integrates concepts of economic development, reduced vulnerability, as well as ecological sustainability, while it simultaneously acknowledges the empowerment of communities from socially and economically deprived contexts. This study envisaged the latter approach as most suitable when understanding sustainable livelihoods.

O. Odularu (✉) · P. Monyai
Department of Development Studies, Faculty of Management and Commerce, University of Fort Hare, Alice, South Africa

G. Odularu (ed.), *Nutrition, Sustainable Agriculture and Climate Change in Africa*,
https://doi.org/10.1007/978-3-030-47875-9_7

The signification that is adopted for purposes of this study is along the following lines: "People's capacities to generate and maintain their means of living, enhance their well-being and that of future generations are contingent upon the availability and accessibility of options which are ecological, economic and political and which are predicated on equity, ownership of resources and participatory in decision-making". The above understanding of sustainable livelihoods highlights the need for community development initiatives to appreciate the capacities of people to manage and cope with the possibilities of risks and uncertainties in doing development. This is useful in realizing and relating factors that hamper and/or boost people's livelihoods, that is, factors that promote capabilities and reduce vulnerabilities. The SL Framework distinguishes between five types of assets or capital upon which livelihoods are built into human, social, natural, physical and economic/financial.[1] For people to be able to enhance their livelihoods, these types of capital have to come into play in interrelated and coordinated ways. This means that they must have access to assets such as personal abilities, tangible assets and financial as well as natural capital. One aspect of capital is social capital. The social capital aspect is linked to the concept of indigenous knowledge systems (IKS), which is defined as "a body of knowledge built up by a group of people through generations of living in close contact". Such knowledge is constantly built and adapted to meet the needs, standards and conditions of local people.

Sustainable development is defined as the management and regulation of the natural ecosystem, societal as well as organizational governance, with a view to providing a reasonable guarantee for the continued survival

[1] Human capital: Comprises knowledge and skills possessed by people, their ability to work and their good health, which makes them able to tackle the varied livelihood strategies to achieve their goals.

Social capital: Include the social resources from which people obtain capacities to assume various livelihood strategies. Social capital includes social relations, networks, associations and affiliations that enable people to define themselves.

Natural capital: Refers to the natural resource base from which people derive a range of necessities for sustainable livelihoods (i.e. which make life possible). These include water, soil and other important natural resources.

Physical capital: Comprises basic infrastructure and other goods necessary for the enhancement of livelihoods.

Economic or financial capital: Refers to the financial resources necessary to support livelihoods. These economic assets range from cash, liquid assets, livestock, income, to any other forms of remittances that can be used to pursue livelihood strategies.

of the generations to come. Sustainable development is therefore about being able to meet today's priorities without compromising the ability of future generations to meet their own basic needs. This implies that sustainable development should afford the equitable opportunity and access for all, including future generations.

The difficulty of with the notion of sustainable development is that it is viewed differently by different people, opening the door for numerous potential complications in how it should be understood and practised. For instance, those who are interested in environmental systems and natural resource conservation often argue for the need to sustain the natural resource base, while others would argue for the need to sustain renewable resources. In addition to the above complexities, communities in developing contexts, particularly in rural areas, often have to depend on the natural resource base in order to satisfy their daily needs. As pointed out earlier, natural resource conservation in such contexts may not be a straightforward matter; it may be marred with complexity and may be a solution that leads to new problems. For instance, it may be difficult to avoid environmental degradation when people are faced with absolute poverty, and the only resource available is from the environment. Lack of knowledge and limited alternatives may leave people with no choice but to sustain themselves through unsustainable means. Such instances have the potential to undermine sustainable development and livelihood and need to be taken into consideration when thinking about sustainable development.

Robert Chambers in 1980s inspired the sustainable livelihood framework, which has been formulated into a conceptual framework by Chambers, Conway and other scholars in the 1990s (DFID 2000: 1–2). Sustainable livelihood approach (SLA) is one of the major theories used to approach the development and poverty analysis by researchers. The SLA uses a conceptual basis along with a set of operational principles to give guidance to policy formulation and development practice. DFID, Oxfam, CARE and UNDP are the proponents of the SLA, and they emphasize and use the approach in various projects and initiatives across the world. The proponents of sustainable livelihood framework use it as a tool for development work to understand, analyse and define the main factors that affect the livelihoods of the poor people. Moreover, DFID (2000) describe a livelihood as "A livelihood comprises the capabilities, assets (including both material and social resources) and activities required for a means of living. A livelihood is sustainable when it can cope with and recover from stresses and shocks, maintain or enhance its capabilities and assets, while not undermining the natural resource base (p., section 1.1)". According to Wong (2015), livelihoods thinking involves a set of activities by pulling out a sort of assets that through intervention processes are translated into livelihoods approaches with the objective to follow a set of livelihoods outcomes. A livelihood is deemed sustainable when it can cope with and recover from stresses and shocks and maintain or enhance its capabilities and assets, while not undermining the natural resource base. They do not only depend on the access to the capital asset but are as well transformed by environmental structures and processes (Wong 2015).

Sustainable livelihood (SL) covers a wide range of topics including the wider discussion regarding the associations of poverty and environmental degradation. It provides an outline that can be used for a variety of diverse measures. Without clarification, there is a risk of simply adding to a conceptual muddle; The major challenge with sustainable livelihood is specifying the "scale of analysis". According to Scoones (1998: 3–4) "in the current literature, there are few explanations about how arguments are tackled, and trade-offs are looked at". The weakness of the sustainable livelihood method is that it starts with a wide-ranging and unrestricted examination which involves a simple analogy which hardly exists. The SL approach is relevant to this study in that it is a holistic and flexible framework for understanding, measuring and analyzing poverty alleviation. The SL approach considers a variety of poverty measures economically, socially, politically and culturally as against some traditional models which measure poverty singly (Scoones 1998; Brock 1999). As the literature suggests, it is always a challenge determining which blend of initiatives is best suited for a specific site, therefore, arriving at "what is a sustainable livelihood among the variety of stakeholders must, therefore, be the first task in any intervention process. As planning for and implementing a sustainable livelihood approach is necessarily interactive and dynamic. It requires the active participation of all the different but interested parties in the processes of defining meanings and objectives, analyzing linkages and trade-offs, identifying options and choices and, ultimately, deciding what to do" (Scoones 1998).

Women Empowerment

It was argued that investing women with economic power was crucial for "sustainable development and the achievement of all Millennium Development Goals" (Raj and Prabhakar 2014). According to Rogerson and Hewitt (2009) empowering women will engender equal access to resources and services and consequently bolster agricultural production, cut down deprivation and encourage rapid economic growth. Duflo (2012) links the empowerment of women to socio-economic growth. Development is seen as playing a complementary role to empowerment and vice versa. According to Duflo, development imbues women with power and with this new-found power women are able to contribute meaningfully in shaping administrative policies and decisions which in turn influences the development process. Nayak and Mahanta (2008) critically examined the state of "women empowerment in India". They used a number of measurements such as women's decision-making power, financial autonomy, political participation etcetera, to assess women status. Their findings suggest that Indian women were comparatively less empowered and ranked low in status compared to their male counterparts despite several interventions by governmental and non-governmental agencies to uplift their status. In their study, which examined the role of development agencies and organizations in the women empowerment processes, Oxaal and Baden (1997) argue that empowering women and involving them in all phases of the development process were essential prerequisites to positive change in any society. Also that promoting women's empowerment (political, economic, legal, physical) should be tailored to meet specific programmes and not treated in isolation.

"Women empowerment came into popularity with the feminist movement whose demand was that women become empowered to take control of their own lives; to set their own agenda of what to do and how to do things that affect them". Women economic empowerment as a course of achieving women's equal access to and control over economic resources and ensuring they can use them to exert improved control over other areas of their lives. More importantly, women empowerment is a construct that comprises cognitive, psychological, economic and political dimensions. The cognitive component entails women's knowledge of the causes of their submissive and marginalization, as well as value the demand to make choices that may go contrary to cultural or social expectation. The psychological component concerns the beliefs and confidence that women can better their condition through personal or collective effort. The economic component describes accessibility to work or vocation or source that provides income independence, while the political component concerns the ability to know one's situation and to mobilize for change.

Government Support/Community Participation

The Government can continue to support sustainable agricultural projects because it is the most reliable project. Women believe that it is reliable and can help alleviate poverty. It is evident that if more of such community projects are established, poverty eradication will surely be enhanced and standard of living and that of the neighbouring environs/communities will be encouraged.

There is a need for awareness and motivation so that younger women can participate as well. Also, women participants are those who have children at home. In order to help them, the government can help alleviate poverty by providing scholarships and funding so that there will be less burden on their parents as regards paying school fees.

Training and educating of females and youths should be encouraged since there is roughly 50% of women, as heads of household, women can be empowered by organizing adult education classes so that they can go to school while their children are in schools. This will enable them to be liberated, informed and independent. The Government can open centres for adult education so that middle-aged women can be encouraged to further their education. This would open opportunities for them including participation in politics, later in life. However, it has been ascertained that CDPs have really helped to liberate women from inequality and poverty in rural areas. However, women should be encouraged to participate in any of the projects they find viable, while the officials and managers overseeing the success of the project give a monthly report of how it is being managed, what needs to be improved on and what needs to focused on. According to the analysis outcome, 50% of the participants had secondary school education. There is a need for government to ensure that the media explains the importance of education continuously through television, radio, a town carrier enlightening woman on education. However, adult day schools are founded across communities. Education is one of the tools of poverty alleviation. The Government can organize various women empowerment lectures in the grass root enlightening women on the importance of education. Opportunities are available for educated women and gender equality.

Community Development, Rural Women, and Socio-Economic Empowerment

Community development is practiced in the underdeveloped, developing and developed countries. The role of women in rural development, food production and poverty, as key agents for development. They play a catalytic role towards the achievement of transformational economic, environmental and social changes required for sustainable development. Despite the challenges they face such as—limited access to credit, health care and education, that are further heightened by the global food and economic crises and climate change. Empowering women is essential, not only for the well-being of individuals, families and rural communities but also for overall economic productivity, given women's large presence in the agricultural workforce worldwide.

UN Women support the leadership and participation of rural women in shaping laws, policies and programmes on all issues that affect their lives, including improved food and nutrition security, and better rural livelihoods. Training equips them with the skills to pursue new livelihoods and adapt technology to their needs. Women play a key role in food production and form a large proportion of the agricultural workforce globally.

Given equal resources, women could contribute much more economically. According to the FAO, if women farmers (43%) of the agricultural labour force in developing countries had the same access as men to finance and decision making, the agricultural output in 34 countries would rise by an estimated average of up to 4%. This could reduce the number of undernourished people in those countries by as much as 17%, translating to up to 150 million fewer hungry people. According to new estimates, about 870 million people (one in eight worldwide) did not consume enough food on a regular basis to cover their minimum dietary energy requirements over the period 2010–2012. The vast majority of them live in developing countries.

To help rural women escape poverty, in 2012, UN Women joined with the World Food Programme, Food and Agriculture Organization, the International Fund for Agriculture Development to launch a joint programme to empower poor rural women through economic integration and food security initiatives. The initiative aims to empower rural women to claim their rights to land, leadership, opportunities. Participation of women in development programmes in the last two decades in the developing world as compared to the developed countries, where, such studies are still very scanty and fragmented are rare; because the role of women in development efforts are hardly acknowledged.

In Ethiopia and Nigeria, some social practices of female seclusion do not allow women to work outside of their homes, in spite of this, women still engage in food processing while the young girls assist in trading. However, technology has played a great role in making food processing easier for women. For instance, for processing cassava, the International Institute of Tropical Agriculture (IITA) provides cassava processors for the women in the villages. This means of processing cassava saves time and also, increases output. The Director-General of the IITA has confirmed that for Nigeria to sustain a developed and equitable agricultural sector, the role of women is the main determining factor.

According to Cary (1983) in Gedze (2012), the objective of the practice of community development should be stemmed from within the community, and not the other way around. Cary's point of view was that people from within the community must take up the dominant platform of community development by partaking significantly. The study recommended proposed that people should learn to acquire skills in those domains where they are willing to take responsibilities in the course of action of community development. Hence, community development could also be determined by the readiness of the prospects both from within and outside the community. However, a proper strength, weaknesses, opportunities and threats (SWOT) analysis within the community and its neighbourhood would be imperative to institute the forms of development programmes required and achievable. Gedze (2012) highlighted that an operative community development programme would necessitate the community not only to draw on its asset but to also take into consideration different ways of assistance accessible outside the community frontiers.

References

Brock, K. (1999). *Implementing from Practice in Mali* (IDS Working Paper 90). Brighton, UK.

Cary, J. L. (1983). *Community Development as a Process*. Columbia: University of Missouri Press.

DFID. (2000). *Framework Introduction. Sustainable Livelihoods Guidance Sheets*. Available at http://www.eldis.org/go/topics/dossiers/livelihoods-connect/what-are-livelihoods-approaches/training-and-learning-materials.

Duflo, E. (2012). *Women's Empowerment and Economic Development* (Working Paper, No. 17702). Cambridge: National Bureau of Economic Research, January 2012.

Gedze, N. (2012). *Government-Sponsored Community Project as Poverty Alleviation Tools? Evidence from Mdantsane, East London*. Mini dissertation, University of Fort Hare, South Africa.

Nayak, P., & Bidisha, M. (2008). *Women Empowerment in India*. Downloaded from http://papers.ssrn.com/sol3/papers.cfm?abstract.id=1320071.

Oxaal, Z., & Baden, S. (1997). *Gender and Empowerment: Definitions, Approaches and Implications for Policy* (Bridge Development-Gender Report, No. 40).

Raj, S., & Prabhakar, R. (2014). Self-Help Group as a Tool of Economic Empowerment of Women. *International Journal of Retailing & Rural Business Perspectives, 3*(1), 829–833.

Scoones, I. (1998). *Sustainable Rural Livelihoods: Whose Reality Counts?* (IDS Discussion Paper 437). Brighton, UK.

Wong, W. (2015). Strengths and Limitations of the Livelihoods Approach, a Bourdieusian Critique.

CHAPTER 8

Agricultural Production, Farm Management, and Greenhouse Gas (GHG) Emissions: Lessons and Policy Directions for Cameroon

Ukpe Udeme Henrietta, Djomo Choumbou Raoul Fani, Ogebe Frank, Gbadebo Odularu, and Oben Njock Emmanuel

U. U. Henrietta
Department of Agricultural Economics and Extension, Federal University Wukari, Wukari, Nigeria

D. C. R. Fani (✉)
Faculty of Agriculture and Veterinary Medicine, Department of Agricultural Economics and Agribusiness, University of Buea, Buea, Cameroon

O. Frank
University of Agriculture, Makurdi, Nigeria

G. Odularu
Department of Economics and Finance, Bay Atlantic University, Washington, DC, USA

O. N. Emmanuel
Department of Agricultural Economics and Agribusiness, University of Buea, Buea, Cameroon

G. Odularu (ed.), *Nutrition, Sustainable Agriculture and Climate Change in Africa*,
https://doi.org/10.1007/978-3-030-47875-9_8

Introduction

The United Nations Commission for the Environment has clearly demonstrated the degradation of the environment both globally and regionally in conjunction with economic activity. This awareness grew stronger at the Rio Summit (Brazil) in 1992 through the acceptance of the concept of sustainable development by the entire international community (Tamba et al. 2012). After the Rio Summit, Cameroon became a member of the United Nations Framework Convention on Climate Change (UNFCCC) in 1994. Thus, Cameroon is committed with the international community to help stabilize concentrations of greenhouse gas (GHG) in the atmosphere to an extent that would prevent dangerous interference of human activities with the climate system (Tamba et al. 2012). The Cameroon government has managed to realize in 1995 inventories of greenhouse gas (GHG) in the energy, industrial, agricultural, land use, and waste sectors (Ministry of Environment and Forests 2005; Tamba et al. 2012). In 1997, a new financial assistance from the Global Environment Facility enabled Cameroon to prepare its first National Communication by developing inventories of greenhouse gas (GHG) emissions with 1994 as a base year. Thus, a first national communication on the GHG inventory in Cameroon was issued to the UNFCCC in 2005 with 2005 as the reference and only year (Ministry of Environment and Forests 2005; Tamba et al. 2012).

Numerous linkages exist between agriculture and climate change. On the one hand, global agriculture is affected by climate change that could significantly impact productivity, especially in the tropics (Lobell et al. 2011; Challinor et al. 2014; Rosenzweig et al. 2014; Stefan et al. 2017). On the other hand, agriculture is an important contributor to climate change, accounting directly for 10–12% of anthropogenic greenhouse gas (GHG) emissions and also for around 70% of land use change emissions, mainly through deforestation (Hosonuma et al. 2012; IPCC 2014; Tubiello et al. 2015; Stefan et al. 2017). Crop and livestock productions directly contribute to the emission of greenhouse gases through the application of nitrogenous fertilizers, responsible for N_2O emissions, and the digestion of ruminants, responsible for emissions. The various ways in which farm wastes are managed (spreading, etc.) also contribute to methane emissions. The crop production sector is responsible for CO_2 emissions both directly, depending on soil management practices, and indirectly through the consumption of intermediate goods (fuel, etc.). On the other hand, like forests, agriculture is also a carbon sink. Conversely, agriculture is highly dependent on climatic conditions (carbon dioxide concentration in the climatic concentration, temperature, hydrological system, stability climatic conditions overtime) which could force production systems to adopt or to move (www.gip-ecofor.org/gicc).

Agricultural emissions from crop and livestock production grew from 4.7 billion tonnes of carbon dioxide equivalents (CO_2 eq) in 2001 to over 5.3 billion tonnes in 2011, the increase occurred mainly in developing countries, due to expansion of total agricultural outputs. Meanwhile, net GHG emissions due to land use change and deforestation registered nearly 10% decrease over 2001–2010 period averaging some 3 billion tonnes CO_2 eq/year over the decade. This was the result of reduced levels of deforestation and increases in the amount of atmospheric carbon being sequestered in many country (www.fao.org/news).

The largest source of GHG emissions within agriculture is entire fermentation when methane is produced by livestock during digestion and released via belches. This accounted in 2011 for 39% of the sector's total GHG outputs. In 2011 44% of agriculture- related GHG outputs occurred in Asia, followed by Americas (25%), Africa (15%), Europe (12%), and Oceania (4%). This regional distribution was fairly constant over the last decade. In 1990 however, Asia's contribution to the global total (38%) was smaller than at present, while Europe's was much larger (21%) (www.fao.org/news).

Although, several studies have been carried out worldwide on the relationship between greenhouse emissions and agriculture (Schneider et al. 2007; Herrero et al. 2013; Valin et al. 2013; Stefan et al. 2017) with little or no emphasis on the linkages between agricultural subsector production, farm management practices, and greenhouse gas (GHG) emissions in Cameroon. Therefore, this study fills the gap in the literature by analyzing the effects of agricultural subsector production and farm management practices on greenhouse gas (GHG) emissions in Cameroon.

Methodology

The Study Area

The study was conducted in Cameroon which has ten regions, namely: Centre; Littoral; Adamawa; Far-North; North; South; East; West; North-West; and South-West. The country covers a total land area of 475,442 sq km and is located in the Central part of Africa within latitudes 2° and 13° North and longitude 9° and 16° East of the equator (United Nations 2004). Cameroon is bordered by Nigeria to the West; Chad to the Northeast; the Central Africa Republic to the East; and Equatorial Guinea, Gabon, and Republic of Congo to the South (World Factsbook 2010).

Method of Data Collection

Due to unavailability of data, annual time series covering a period of 34 years (1980–2013) were obtained from World Bank development indicators data base and Ministry of Environment.

Techniques of Data Analysis

Augmented Dikey Fuller test (ADF) was used for stationary test of variables. Johansen Cointegration test used to test the existence of long run relationship among variables. Vector error correction model was used to analyse the broad objective of this study. Variance decomposition was used to examine contribution of agricultural subsector production and farm management practices on GHG and impulse response was used to examine the response of GHG to agricultural subsector production and farm management practices.

Model Specification

Augmented Dikey Fuller Test (ADF)

Following Oyinbo and Rekwot (2014) the Augmented Dickey Fuller (ADF) model with the constant term and trend can be specified as follows:

$$\Delta Y_t = \alpha_0 + \alpha_1 t + \beta Y_{t-1} + \sum_{i=1}^{p} \delta_i \Delta Y_{t-i} + \varepsilon_t \tag{1}$$

where Υ is the value of the variable of interest (agricultural labor force, government expenditures on research and development, education and health), α_0 is the constant, α_1 is the coefficient of the trend series, p is the lag order of the autoregressive process, Y_{t-1} is lagged value of order one of Y_{t-1} and ε_t is the error term.

Johansen Cointegration Test

A linear combination of two or more $I(1)$ series may be stationary or $I(0)$, in which case the series are co-integrated. The null hypothesis for the Johansen Cointegration test ($H!$: $r = 0$) implies that cointegration does not exist, while the alternative hypothesis ($H!$: $r > 0$) implies that it does. If the null for non-cointegration is rejected, the lagged residual from the co-integrating regression is imposed as the error correction term in a Vector Error Correction Model (VECM) given below as:

$$\nabla Y_t = \prod Y_{t-1} + \sum_{i=1}^{k-1} \tau_i \nabla Y_{t-1} + u + \varepsilon_t \tag{2}$$

where ∇Y_t = First difference of a $(n \times i)$ vector of the n variables of interest, $\prod = (n \times n)$ Coefficient matrix associated with lagged values of the endogenous dependent variables, Y_{t-1} = Lagged values of $Y_t, \tau = (n \times (k-1))$ Matrix of short term coefficients, u = $(n \times 1)$ Vector of constant and $\varepsilon_t = (n \times 1)$ Vector of White Noise Residuals

Vector Error Correction Model (VECM)

$$\begin{aligned} \ln Y_{t-i} &= a_0 + a_1 \ln CP_{t-i} + a_2 \ln LV_{t-i} + a_3 \ln FC_{t-i} \\ &\quad + a_4 \ln AGL_{t-i} + ECM_t + u_t \end{aligned} \tag{3}$$

where

- Y_{t-i} GHG (Mt of CO_2 equivalent)
- CP_{t-i} crop production index (2004–2006 = 100)
- LV_{t-i} livestock production index (2004–2006 = 100)
- FC_{t-i} fertilizer consumption (kg/hectare)
- AGL_{t-i} agricultural land use (hectare)
- ECM_t error correction term
- u_t error term.

Results and Discussion

The result in Table 8.1 presents the summary of unit root tests conducted under the ADF at level and first difference. The result indicates all the variables (GHG, Livestock, Crop, Agricultural Land use, and fertilizer consumption were stationary at first difference at 1 and 5% level of significance. Therefore, by analyzing the table it shows that all the variables were stationary at first difference and are therefore characterized as I(1) process.

The unrestricted cointegration test is based on the Trace Statistic at 5% level of significance is presented in Table 8.2. The result shows that Trace

Table 8.1 Unit root test (ADF TEST)

	ADF results				
	At level		*At first difference*		*Decision*
Variables	t-*statistic*	*Probability*	t-*statistic*	*Probability*	
GHG	−1.14	0.68	−5.87	0.000***	I(1)
Livestock	0.55	0.98	−6.46	0.000***	I(1)
Crop	−0.009	0.99	−5.35	0.000***	I(1)
Agric land	−0.59	0.97	−3.80	0.029**	I(1)
Fertilizer	−2.66	0.25	−6.18	0.000***	I(1)

Note N.B*** and **indicate stationary at 1 and 5% level of significance, respectively
Source Author's creation

Table 8.2 Johansen cointegration test

Unrestricted cointegration rank test (trace)				
Hypothesized No. of CE(s)	*Eigenvalue*	*Trace Statistic*	*0.05 Critical value*	*Prob.***
None*	0.701217	73.93010	69.81889	0.0226
At most 1	0.397241	36.48089	47.85613	0.3724
At most 2	0.339402	20.78750	29.79707	0.3710
At most 3	0.218687	7.934614	15.49471	0.4724
At most 4	0.009134	0.284451	3.841466	0.5938

Source Author's creation
Note Trace test indicates 1 cointegrating eqn(s) at the 0.05 level, *denotes rejection of the hypothesis at the 0.05 level, **MacKinnon-Haug-Michelis (1999) *p*-values

Statistic value (73.93) is greater than the critical value (69.81) implying the presence of cointegration which indicates the long run relationship among variables. But in the subsequent cointegration equation, critical values are greater than the Trace Statistic implying the rejection of the null hypothesis that there is cointegration. Trace statistic value test indicates one (1) co-integrating equations at 5% level of significance.

The result of the effect of agricultural subsector output and farm management practices on greenhouse gas emissions is presented in Table 8.3. The result shows that the coefficient of determination (R^2) is 0.47 implying that 47% of the variation of greenhouse gas emissions (GHG) is explained by crop subsector production, livestock subsector production, fertilizer consumption, and agricultural land use. The result also shows that F-statistic (3.64) was significant at 1% level indicating the goodness of fit and overall significance of variables used in the model. Further, the result shows that crop subsector production in the previous year, livestock subsector production in the previous year, and fertilizer consumption in the previous year were the variables that significantly affected GHG in the long run. Specifically, the coefficients of crop subsector production in the previous year (−2.56) and fertilizer consumption in the previous year (−0.22) were negative and significant at 1 and 5% level. This implies that a unit increase in crop subsector production in the previous year and fertilizer consumption in the previous year will decrease GHG by 2.56 and 0.22%, respectively. In contrast, the coefficient of livestock subsector production in the previous year (3.03) was positive and significant at 1%. This implies that a unit increase in livestock subsector production in the previous year will increase GHG by 3.03%. However, the coefficient of agricultural land use was not significant indicating that agricultural land in the previous year use has no significant effect on GHG in the long run.

In the short run, the result shows that GHG in the previous year was the only variable that affects significantly GHG. Specifically, the coefficient of GHG in the previous year (0.55) was positive and significant at 5% level. This implies that a unit increase in GHG in the previous year will increase GHG by 0.55% in the short run. However, the coefficients of fertilizer consumption in the previous year, crop subsector production in the previous year, livestock subsector production in the previous year, and agricultural land use in the previous year were not significant. Therefore, they have no significant effect on GHG in the short run.

Table 8.3 Effect of agricultural subsector production and farm management practices on greenhouse gas emissions

Cointegrating Eq:	*CointEq1*			
LNGHG(−1)	1.000000			
LNFERTILIZER(−1)	−0.22** [−2.16]			
LNLIVESTOCK(−1)	3.03*** [8.30]			
LNCROP(−1)	−2.56*** [−8.99]			
LNAGRLAND(−1)	−1.83[−0.47]			
C	−4.550980			
Error correction:	D(LNGHG)	D(LNFERTILIZER)	D(LNLIVESTOCK)	D(LNCROP)
CointEq1	−1.30[−4.24]	0.45[2.03]	−0.01[−0.70]	0.08[2.17]
D(LNGHG(−1))	0.55**[2.40]	−0.01[−0.11]	0.01[0.61]	−0.01[−0.44]
D(LNFERTILIZER(−1))	−0.14[−0.53]	−0.33[−1.77]	−0.01[−0.54]	−0.03[−1.01]
D(LNLIVESTOCK(−1))	2.44[1.16]	−0.60[−0.40]	−0.04[−0.24]	−0.01[−0.06]
D(LNAGRLAND(−1))	−10.14[−0.80]	1.95[0.21]	1.22[1.07]	0.28[0.17]
C	−0.06[−0.56]	−0.04[−0.48]	0.03[3.59]	0.03[2.54]
R^2	0.47	0.31	0.14	0.27
Adj. R^2	0.34	0.14	−0.06	0.09
Sum sq. resids	3.82	1.98	0.03	0.06

Cointegrating Eq:	*CointEq1*			
S.E. equation	0.39	0.28	0.03	0.05
F-statistic	3.64***	1.85	0.68	1.50
Log likelihood	−11.53	−1.37	62.91	51.71
Akaike AIC	1.19	0.54	−3.60	−2.88
Schwarz SC	1.51	0.86	−3.28	−2.56
Mean dependent	0.009	−0.01	0.03	0.03
S.D. dependent	0.49	0.31	0.03	0.05
Determinant resid covariance (dof adj.)		1.08E-12		
Determinant resid covariance		2.99E-13		
Log likelihood		227.0537		
Akaike information criterion		−12.06798		
Schwarz criterion		−10.21767		

Note N.B.*** and **are significant at 1 and 5% Values in bracket are *t*-statistics
Source Author's creation

The Response of Greenhouse Gas Emissions to Agricultural Subsector production and farm management Practices is presented in Fig. 8.1. The graph shows that Greenhouse Gas Emissions respond positively to a unit shock throughout the period. Similarly, the graph also shows that greenhouse gas emissions respond positively to unit shock of crop subsector production and fertilizer consumption, respectively. In contrast, the graph

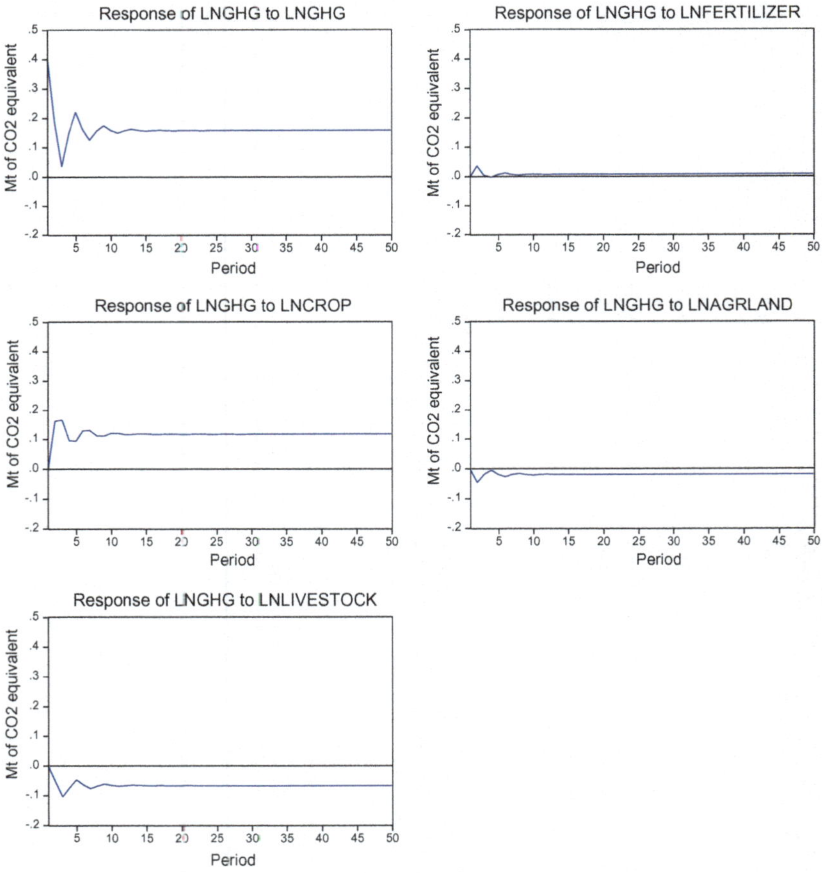

Fig. 8.1 Response of greenhouse gas emissions to agricultural subsector production and farm management practices

shows that greenhouse gas emissions respond negatively to unit shock of livestock subsector production and agricultural land use, respectively.

Variance Decomposition for Greenhouse Gas Emissions in the Five Decades (50 Years)

The contribution of Agricultural Subsector production and farm management Practices to Greenhouse Gas Emissions is presented in Table 8.4. The result shows that in the short run (5 years) greenhouse gas emissions will contribute to itself for 73.14%. Crop subsector production will contribute for 20.17%. Livestock subsector production will contribute for 5.56%. Fertilizer consumption will contribute for 0.43% and agricultural land use will contribute for 0.68%. In the next decade (10 years), greenhouse gas emissions will contribute to itself for 66.56%. Crop subsector production will contribute for 25.5%. Livestock subsector production will contribute for 7.08%. Fertilizer consumption will contribute for 0.36% and agricultural land will contribute for 0.72%. In the next two decades (20 years), greenhouse gas emissions will contribute to itself for 62.59%. Crop subsector production will contribute for 28.25%. Livestock subsector production will contribute for 8.14%. Fertilizer consumption will contribute for 0.29% and agricultural land use will contribute for 0.70%. In the next three decades (30 years), greenhouse gas emissions will contribute to itself for 61.07%. Crop subsector production will contribute for 29.41%. Livestock subsector production will contribute for 8.53%. Fertilizer consumption will contribute for 0.26% and agricultural land use

Table 8.4 Contribution of agricultural subsector production and farm management practices to greenhouse gas emissions

Period	*S.E.*	*GHG*	*Crop*	*Livestock*	*Agric land use*	*Fertilizer consumption*
5	0.60	73.14	20.17	5.56	0.68	0.43
10	0.76	66.56	25.25	7.08	0.72	0.36
20	1.01	62.59	28.25	8.14	0.70	0.29
30	1.21	61.07	29.41	8.53	0.69	0.26
40	1.38	60.26	30.04	8.75	0.69	0.25
50	1.53	59.74	30.43	8.88	0.68	0.24

Source Author's creation

will contribute for 0.69%. In the next four decades (40 years), greenhouse gas emissions will contribute to itself for 60.26%. Crop subsector production will contribute for 30.04%. Livestock subsector production will contribute for 8.75%. Fertilizer consumption will contribute for 0.25% and agricultural land use will contribute for 0.69%. In the next five decades (50 years), greenhouse gas emissions will contribute to itself for 59.74%. Crop subsector production will contribute for 30.43%. Livestock subsector production will contribute for 8.88%. Fertilizer consumption will contribute for 0.24% and agricultural land use will contribute for 0.68%.

Conclusion and Recommendations

This study analyzed the effects of agricultural subsector production and farm management practices on greenhouse gas emissions in Cameroon (1980–2013). It was found that the agricultural subsector production in the previous year (crop and livestock) and farm management practices in the previous year (fertilizer consumption and agricultural land use) significantly affect GHG in the long run while GHG in the previous year significantly affect itself in the short run. The result also shows that GHG respond positively to a unit shock of crop subsector production and fertilizer consumption while GHG respond negatively to a unit shock of livestock subsector production and agricultural land use. Finally, crop subsector production is the major contributor to GHG in both long and short run. It is therefore recommended that:

(i) Integrated farming system should be practiced with emphasis on organic farming since crop subsector production has significant effect on GHG in Cameroon.
(ii) Given that livestock subsector production increases GHG, animal feed and manure management (collection, storage, and utilisation) should be appropriately handled to meet up with the scientific requirement.
(iii) Policy on land tenure system should also be set up through appropriate laws in order to reduce the over utilisation of agricultural land.

References

Challinor, A. J., Watson, J., Lobell, D. B., Howden, S. M., Smith, D. R., & Chhetri, N. (2014). A Meta-Analysis of Crop Yield Under Climate Change and Adaptation. *Nature Climate Change, 4,* 287–291.

Herrero, M., Havlík, P., Valin, H., Notenbaert, A., Rufino, M. C., Thornton, P. K., et al. (2013). Biomass Use, Production, Feed Efficiencies, and Greenhouse Gas Emissions from Global Livestock Systems. *Proceedings of the National Academy of Sciences, 110,* 20888–20893.

Hosonuma, N., Herold, M., De Sy, V., De Fries, R. S., Brockhaus, M., Verchot, L., et al. (2012). An Assessment of Deforestation and Forest Degradation Drivers in Developing Countries. *Environmental Research Letters, 7,* 044009.

IPCC. (2014). *Climate Change 2014: Mitigation of Climate Change* (Contribution of Working Group III to the Fifth Assessment Report of the Intergovernmental Panel on Climate Change). Cambridge, NY: Cambridge University Press.

Lobell, D. B., Schlenker, W., & Costa-Roberts, J. (2011). Climate Trends and Global Crop Production Since 1980. *Science, 333,* 616–620.

MacKinnon, J. G., Haug, A. A., & Michelis, L. (1999). Numerical Distribution Functions of Likelihood Ratio Tests for Cointegration. *Journal of Applied Econometrics, 14*(5), 563–577. https://doi.org/10.1002/(SICI)1099-1255(199909/10)14:5<563::AID-JAE530>3.0.CO;2-R.

Ministry of Environment and Forests. (2005). *Cameroon Initial National Communication to UNFCCC.* http://unfccc.int/resource/docs/natc/cmrnc1f.

Oyinbo, O., & Rekwot, G. Z. (2014). The Relationships of Inflationary Trend, Agricultural Productivity and Economic Growth in Nigeria. *CBN Journal of Applied Statistics, 5*(1), 35–47.

Rosenzweig, C., Elliot, J., Deryng, D., Ruange, A. C., Muller, C., Arneth, A., et al. (2014). Assessing Agricultural Risks of Climate Change in the 21st Century in a Global Gridded Crop Model Intercomparison. *Proceedings of the National Academy of Sciences, 111,* 3268–3273.

Schneider, U. A., McCarl, B. A., & Schmid, E. (2007). Agricultural Sector Analysis on Greenhouse Gas Mitigation in US Agriculture and Forestry. *Agricultural Systems, 94,* 128–140.

Stefan, F., PetrHavl, K., Soussana, J.F., Levesque, A., Valin, H., Wollenberg, E., et al. (2017). Reducing Greenhouse Gas Emissions in Agriculture without Compromising Food Security? *Environmental Research Letters, 12,* 105004.

Tamba, J. G., Njomo, D., Nsouandele, J. L., Bonoma, B., & Dongue, S. B. (2012). Assessment of Greenhouse Gas Emissions in Cameroon's Road Transport Sector. *Universal Journal of Environmental Research and Technology, 2*(6), 475–488.

Tubiello, F. N., Salvatore, M., Ferrara, A. F., Jo, H., Federici, S., Rossi, S., et al. (2015). The Contribution of Agriculture Forestry and Other Land Use Activities to Global Warming, 1990–2012. *Global Change Biology, 21*, 2655–2660.

United Nations. (2004). *Demographic Year Book* (500pp). Statistics Division.

Valin, H., Havlík, P., Mosnier, A., Herrero, M., Schmid, E., & Obersteiner, M. (2013). Agricultural Productivity and Greenhouse Gas Emissions: Trade-Offs or Synergies Between Mitigation and Food Security? *Environmental Research Letters, 8*, 035019.

World Factsbook. (2010). *Cameroon Economy*. www.cia.gov/cia/publication/factsbook/goes/htm. Retrieved on 10 November 2015.

www.fao.org/news. Accessed on 26 December 2017.

www.gip-ecofor.org/gicc. Accessed on 26 December 2017.

CHAPTER 9

Productivity Analysis Among Smallholder Rice Farmers: Policy Implications for Nutrition Security in the West Region of Cameroon

Djomo Choumbou Raoul Fani, Ukpe Udeme Henrietta, Oben Njock Emmanuel, and Gbadebo Odularu

D. C. R. Fani (✉)
Faculty of Agriculture and Veterinary Medicine, Department of Agricultural Economics and Agribusiness, University of Buea, Buea, Cameroon

U. U. Henrietta
Department of Agricultural Economics and Extension, Federal University Wukari, Wukari, Nigeria

O. N. Emmanuel
Department of Agricultural Economics and Agribusiness, University of Buea, Buea, Cameroon

G. Odularu
Department of Economics and Finance, Bay Atlantic University, Washington, DC, USA

G. Odularu (ed.), *Nutrition, Sustainable Agriculture and Climate Change in Africa*,
https://doi.org/10.1007/978-3-030-47875-9_9

Introduction

With recent development in the Cameroon's agricultural policy, small scale farmers have become the central focus due to the fact that the nation's agriculture has always been dominated by small scale farmers, who represent substantial proportion of the total population and produce an overwhelming 93% of total output with average farm size of 1–2 hectares (Piebeb 2008). The implication is that there is a scope for additional increase in domestic output from existing hectares if efficiency of rice production is improved. In Cameroon, the agricultural sector employs over 60% of the active population; ensures a large share of the country's food security; generates foreign exchange receipts (up to 55% of export receipts) and contributes up to 20% of gross domestic product (GDP) (Amadou 2007; Dontsop et al. 2009; Gama 2013; Djomo 2015). Moreover, agricultural activity induces most of the spread effects on other sectors of the economy; thus contributing to export diversification, job creation and poverty reduction (INS 2005; Dontsop et al. 2009).

Despite agriculture's enormous contributions to the Cameroonian economy over the years, the performance of this sector has been low in recent years. For instance, the average contribution of Cameroon's agricultural sector to GDP was 30% before the advent of crude oil in 1978. The share of agriculture in GDP declined to 24% in 1987, then increased to 27% in 1990 (Gbetnkom and Khan 2002; Bamou and Masters 2007; Gama 2013) and decreased to 19.8% in 2010 (World Factsbook 2010; Gama 2013). Reasons pointed out by economic literature for the poor performance includes, among others, the decline in primary commodity prices; the appreciation of franc CFA (FCFA) relative to the US Dollar and certain domestic distortions, such as the high costs of inputs, the cumbersomeness of the administrative machinery and the poor management of public enterprises (Amadou 2007; Dontsop et al. 2009; Gama 2013).

However, until 1980s rice was still regarded as a foreign crop and was only consumed during special events of the year. Rice has gradually become a staple food for rural and urban populace in Cameroon. The consumption of rice has increased faster than other food crops and according to projections at the national and international level, this is likely to continue for some time (MINAGRI 2002; ACDIC 2006; Piebeb 2008). Yet, rice is one of the most important crops in the world after wheat, yet consumption is growing at an annual rate of 4% and was estimated at 25.9 kg per caput in 2008 (MINADER 2008). In order to boost rice production and farmers ability to increase their earnings (profitability) in Cameroon, three development companies were created by the Cameroonian government, namely: *the Societe d'Expansion et de Modernisation de Riziculture de Yagoua (SEMRY)* in 1954; the Upper Noun Valley Development Authority (UNVDA) in 1974 and *the Societe de Development de la Riziculture dans la plaine de Mbo (SODERIM)* in 1978. Despite these magnitudes of investment, Cameroon produces an estimated 80,000 metric tonnes of rice annually of which the West Region accounts for about 20%. This is far short of the over 500,000 metric tonnes required to meet national demand (MINAGRI 2002; Piebeb 2008; Djomo 2015).

Moreover, the demand of rice today exceeds production and large quantities of rice are imported to meet the country's requirement at huge expenses in terms of foreign exchange. Nevertheless, world production indicated that Cameroon had one of the greatest increases in production between 1961 and 2005 with an expansion of over 1500% (FAO 2006; Piebeb 2008). Although this figure looks significant, the record, however, is one of stability rather than growth. The Cameroonian population has grown faster than total production (World Bank 2007; Piebeb 2008).

There has been a remarkable importation of rice in recent years. Therefore, a strategy of accelerating production should explore the potentials of this cash crop by analyzing technical efficiency of small scale rice farmers which will culminate into incremental rice output, profitability and sustainability of the rice crop enterprise. Although, rice contributes a significant proportion of the food requirements of the population in Cameroon; production capacity is still far below the national requirement. To meet the increasing demand, the importation of milled rice is used to bridge the gap, and as a result, Cameroon spends at least 100 billion fcfa (about 209 million USD) annually to import the estimated 500,000 metric tons of rice needed for households (Ministry of Agriculture and Rural Development 2009). FAO (2006), Piebeb (2008) reported that Cameroon was one of the countries that witnessed the most prevalent and frequent food import surges for the period 1999–2003, with rice identified as the most affected commodity. This study identified and estimates sources of inefficiency of small scale rice farmers which provide information to government, students and researchers on how socioeconomic variables influenced input utilization. Also the efficiency estimates provide the level at which small scale rice farmers utilized the available resources which guide extension officers and nongovernmental organizations on resource use efficiency in the study area.

Several studies have been carried out on rice in Cameroon, such as: ACDIC (2006) analysis on food sovereignty in Cameroon was based on the rice sector; Fonjong and Mbah (2007) analyzed the fortunes and misfortunes of women rice producers in Ndop-Cameroon: the implications for gender roles; Piebeb (2008) evaluated the constraints and opportunities for sustainable rice production and also reviewed rice production in Cameroon. Ministry of Agriculture and Rural Development (2009), focussed on the national strategy for rice growing in Cameroon; Molua (2010) studied the response of rice yields in Cameroon: implication for agricultural price policy; rice production response to trade liberalization; price and non price determinants and acreage response of rice in Cameroon; and Bime et al. (2014) analyzed profitability and marketing channels of rice in Menchum River Valley of North West Region of Cameroon. Also studies have been done on efficiency in Cameroon such as: Binam et al. (2005) who analyzed sources of technical efficiency among smallholder maize and peanut farmers in the slash and burn agriculture zone of Cameroon. Amadou (2007) who analyzed factors affecting efficiency of Arabica coffee farmers in Cameroon; Dontsop et al. (2009) identified determinants of cocoa farmers in Centre Province of Cameroon; Gama (2013) analyzed productivity and economic efficiency of cocoa farmers in South West Region of Cameroon. Nevertheless, few studies investigated productivity among smallholder farmers in rice with emphasis on the technical efficiency and profitability in the West Region of Cameroon. It has, therefore, become imperative to undertake this study to empirically document productivity analysis among smallholder rice farmers and its Policy implications for nutrition security in the West Region of Cameroon.

Methodology

The Study Area

The study was conducted in the West Region of Cameroon which has eight divisions, namely: Bamboutos, Haut-Nkam, Mifi, Menoua, Khoung-khi, Nde, Noun and Hauts-Plateaux. The West Region covers a total land area of 14,000 sq km and is located in the West-Central part of Cameroon within latitudes 5° 20′ and 7° North and longitude

9° 40′ and 11° 10′ East of the equator (Yerima and Van 2005). The West Region of Cameroon is 300 m above sea level. It is characterized by two main seasons: dry season from November to mid-March and rainy season from mid-March to October. The annual rainfall varies between 1300 and 3000 mm with a mean of 2000 mm. The region has a minimum and maximum temperature of 15.5 and 24.5 °C, respectively (Yerima and Van 2005).

Population and Sampling Procedure

The population of the study comprised all the small scale rice farmers in the West Region of Cameroon, which include: Noun, Nde, Bamboutos, Mifi, Menoua, Haut-Nkam, Hauts-Plateaux and Koung-Khi. Since it is impractical and uneconomic to obtain information from the entire population, a sample of the population was taken by adopting a multistage selection involving purposive and stratified random sampling procedure. First, four divisions were purposively selected (Bamboutos, Nde, Noun, and Menoua) based on the high concentration of rice production in those divisions. The second stage involved a random selection of one subdivision from each of the selected divisions, namely: Tonga in Nde division, Foumbot in Noun division, Santchou in Menoua division and Galim in Bamboutos division. The third stage of the sampling process involved a random selection of one community in each of the selected subdivisions namely: Keneghang, Babitchoua, Baigom and Sekou. Given the total number of farmers in these communities, a proportional sample of 8% of small scale rice farmers was randomly selected in each community. Thus a total of 192 small scale rice farmers were selected for the study. The sample size selection is presented more explicitly in Table 9.1.

Data Collection Techniques

This study involved the collection of data from primary sources. Primary data were collected through structured questionnaires and interview scheduled which were administered to the sampled small scale rice farmers with the aid of enumerators who serve as extension officer.

Table 9.1 Sample size selection (sampling proportion at 8%)

Divisions	*Subdivisions*	*Communities*	*Sample frame*	*Sampling proportion*	*Sample size*
Bamboutos	Galim	Keneghang	750	0.08	60
Nde	Tonga	Babitchoua	650	0.08	52
Noun	Foumbot	Baigom	450	0.08	36
Menoua	Santchou	Sekou	550	0.08	44
Total	4	4	2400	0.08	192

Source Field Survey, 2014

Validation and Reliability of Instrument

The research instrument was validated by pilot testing and by passing it through my supervisors, to ensure that it possesses both face and content validity. The reliability of the instrument was conducted using a test-retest method. In doing this, twenty (20) questionnaires were administered twice to two communities drawn from the sample frame within the interval of two weeks. The scores ($r = 0.75$) obtained were correlated using Pearson Product moment correlation coefficient(r) indicating a high correlation.

Data Analysis Techniques

Stochastic frontier production function and gross margin analysis were used to assess technical efficiency and profitability, respectively.

Model Specifications

Technical Efficiency Model

The Cobb–Douglas stochastic production frontier model can be stated as:

$$\begin{aligned} \text{LnY} = \beta_0 + \beta_1\text{LnX}_1 + \beta_2\text{LnX}_2 + \beta_3\text{LnX}_3 \\ + \beta_4\text{LnX}_4 + \beta_5\text{LnX}_5 + \beta_6\text{LnX}_6 + \text{V}_1 - \text{U}_1 \end{aligned} \quad (1)$$

where

Ln = Natural logarithm to base 10

Y = Total rice output of the farmer in kilogram per hectare (kg/ha)

βs = The parameters to be estimated

X_1 = Farm size in hectares

X_2 = Labour used measured in mandays per hectare

X_3 = Quantity of improved seeds planted in kilogram per hectare (kg/ha)

X_4 = Quantity of fertilizers applied measured in kilogram per hectare (kg/ha)

X_5 = Quantity of pesticides used measured in litres per hectare (litres/ha)

X_6 = Quantity of herbicides used measured in litres per hectare (litres/ha)

V_1 = Random errors which are assumed to be independently and identically distributed

U_1 = Non negative random variable associated with technical inefficiency of production.

This is assumed to be independently distributed such that U_1 is obtained by truncation (at zero) of the normal distribution with variance δ^2 and mean U_1.

The inefficiency of production was modelled in terms of factors such as

$$U_1 = \sigma_0 + \sigma_1 Z_1 + \sigma_2 Z_2 + \sigma_3 Z_3 + \sigma_4 Z_4 + \sigma_5 Z_5 + \sigma_6 Z_6 + \sigma_7 Z_7 \quad (2)$$

where

σ = a vector of unknown parameters to be estimated

Z_1 = age of farmers in years

Z_2 = Level of Education measured in number of years spent in formal education

Z_3 = number of years of farming experience in rice production

Z_4 = household size measured as number of family member living together in a house

Z_5 = rice variety (improved variety = 1, local variety = 0)

Z_6 = Extension contact (number of extension contact in a year)

Z_7 = Access to credit (amount in fcfa).

Gross Margin Analysis

Gross Margin is given as:

$$GM = TR - TVC$$

where

GM = Gross margin (fcfa/hectare)
TR = Total Revenue (fcfa/hectare)
TVC = Total Cost (fcfa/hectare).

Results and Discussion

The effect of input (farm size, labour, quantity of seeds, quantity of fertilizer, quantity of pesticides and quantity of herbicides) on output obtained estimate from the stochastic production function of small scale rice farmers is summarized in Table 9.1.

The result indicates that farm size, labour use and fertilizer were the inputs that significantly affect the rice output. Specifically, farm size and labour use were found positive and significantly influence rice output of farmers at 5% level of probability. This is close to the research finding by Umeh and Ataborh (2011) who found that farm size and labour use by Nigerians' rice farmers were significant at 5%. This implies that increases in farm size and labour use by one unit will also increase rice output by the value of their coefficients, respectively. In contrast, the coefficient of fertilizer was negative and significant at 5% level of probability. This result agrees with the findings of Ahmadu and Erhabor (2012) who found that the estimated coefficient of quantity of fertilizer use by rice farmers in Taraba State, Nigeria was negative. The negative and significant coefficient of fertilizer implies that increases in fertilizer application will reduce the output of rice by the value of its coefficient. The result suggests that small scale rice farmers in the West Region of Cameroon misapplied fertilizer in the West Region of Cameroon. However, the estimated coefficients for seeds, pesticides and herbicides used were not significant.

The return to scale is 0.51 with respect to farm size, labour and quantity of fertilizer used, which is positive. Technically small scale rice farmers are in rational stage of their production surface as the output is increasing at decreasing rate relative to quantity of input use. This also implies that 1% increase in all inputs lead to 0.51% increase of output.

The result of estimated parameters of the inefficiency effects models of small scale rice producers in the West Region of Cameroon showed that the estimated sigma square (σ^2) is significant at 5% level of probability for small scale rice farmers indicating goodness of fit and correctness of the specified distribution assumption of the composite error terms. The estimated gamma (Γ) is significant at 5% implying that 3.3% of the variability in small scale rice output is due to technical inefficiency. The estimated coefficients of technical inefficiency effects model in Table 9.5 indicate that extension contact and access to credit significantly influenced technical inefficiency of small scale rice farmer's in the West Region of Cameroon. However, age, education, experience, household size and rice variety have no influence on technical inefficiency of smallholder rice farmers in the study area. The Coefficients of extension contact and access to credit were, respectively negative and positive and significant at 5% level of probability. The implication is that technical inefficiency effects in small scale rice production in the West Region of Cameroon declined with increase in extension contacts. In order words, farmer's contact with extension agents in the West Region of Cameroon has positive effects on technical efficiency in small scale rice production. It is therefore important for achieving effective utilization of inputs in small scale rice production in the West Region of Cameroon. In addition, this is an indication that knowledge and orientation on agricultural technologies from extension contacts have strong influence on technical efficiency, following Dimelu et al. (2009) and Simonyan et al. (2011). As for access to credit, the implication of the result is that technical inefficiency effects in small scale rice production increases with increase in access to credit. The result suggests that small scale rice farmers' misused credit obtained from financial institutions. It is therefore not important for achieving efficient use of inputs in small scale rice production. In other words access to credit by smallholder rice farmers contribute to achieve lower level of technical efficiency. This is contrary to the findings of Dontsop et al. (2009) and Amadou (2007) who found that access to credit decreases technical inefficiency of cocoa and Arabica coffee farmers, respectively in Cameroon.

Efficiency Estimates of Small Scale Rice Farmers in the West Region of Cameroon

The technical efficiency estimates of small scale rice farmers in the West Region of Cameroon is summarized in Table 9.2. The result indicates that small scale rice farmers in the West Region of Cameroon had technical efficiency varying from 65 to 99% with the mean of 82%. This implies that technical efficiency in small scale rice production in the West Region of Cameroon could be increased by 18% through efficient use of available resources given the current state of technology and this could be achieved through better extension contacts. This result is however; above

Table 9.2 Maximum likelihood estimates of production function of small scale rice farmers in the West Region of Cameroon

Variables	*Coefficients*	*Estimated value of coefficients*
Constant	β_0	6.558 (11.11*)
Farm size	β_1	0.277 (4.44*)
Labour	β_2	0.426 (4.91*)
Quantity of seeds	β_3	0.127 (1.35)
Quantity of fertilizer	β_4	−0.193 (−2.33*)
Quantity of pesticides	β_5	0.161 (1.09)
Quantity of herbicides	β_6	−0.556 (−0.48)
Inefficiency factors		
Constant	Z_0	0.057 (0.13)
Age	Z_1	0.070 (0.66)
Education	Z_2	8.143 (0.43)
Experience	Z_3	−0.020 (−0.84)
Household size	Z_4	−0.021 (−0.33)
Rice variety	Z_5	−0.070 (−1.56)
Extension contact	Z_6	−0.078 (−5.11*)
Access to credit	Z_7	9.023 (2.32*)
Sigma square	σ^2	0.063 (9.54*)
Gamma	Γ	0.033 (2.57*)
Log likelihood function		−8.13
LR test	LR	28.64*

Note *Significant at 5% figures in bracket are *t* values
Source Field Survey, 2014

the findings of Binam et al. (2005) who found the average technical efficiency of 77, 78 and 80%, respectively for maize/groundnut intercrop systems, groundnut monocrop and maize monocrop in Cameroon. Specifically, 9.4% of small scale rice farmers had technical efficiency of 0.61–0.70; 38.5% of small scale rice farmers had technical efficiency of 0.71–0.80; 31.8% had technical efficiency of 0.81–0.90 and finally, 20.3% had technical efficiency of 0.91–1.

Gross Margin Analysis of Small Scale Rice Production in the West Region of Cameroon

Gross margin analysis in small scale rice production in the West Region of Cameroon is summarized in Table 9.3. The result indicates that the mean cost incurred on labour constitutes 43.73% of the average total variable cost. The result further revealed that the mean cost of seeds constitutes 18.65% of the average total variable cost. The result also revealed that the mean cost of pesticides constitutes 3.63% of the average total variable cost. Similarly the mean cost of herbicides constitutes 8.89% of the average total variable cost and the mean cost of fertilizer constitutes 25.16% of the average total variable cost. The mean revenue is 394,000 FCFA which means that, on the average small scale rice farmer obtained a gross margin of 67,000 FCFA/ha. This value when compared with the value (134,484.9 FCFA/ha) obtained by Bime et al. (2014) in their study on analysis of profitability and marketing channels of rice in Menchum River Valley of North-West Region of Cameroon shows a decreases in profitability which may be attributed to inability of small scale rice farmers in the West Region of Cameroon to minimize cost incurred during the production process and besides the average yields per hectare in the West Region is slightly lower (2.8 t/ha compare to 3.2 t/ha (Ministry of Agriculture and Rural Development 2009) (Table 9.4).

Table 9.3 Distribution of respondents by efficiency estimates of small scale rice farmers in the West Region of Cameroon

Technical efficiency	*Frequency*	*Percentage (%)*
0.61–0.70	18	9.4
0.71–0.80	74	38.5
0.81–0.90	61	31.8
0.91–1	39	20.3
Total	192	100
Maximum	0.99	
Minimum	0.65	
Mean	0.82	

Source Field Survey, 2014

Table 9.4 Descriptive statistics of cost and return variables of small scale rice farmers in the West Region of Cameroon

Statistics	*Cost of labour (fcfa/ha)*	*Cost of seeds (fcfa/ha)*	*Cost of pesticides (fcfa/ha)*	*Cost of herbicides (fcfa/ha)*	*Cost of fertilizer (fcfa/ha)*	*Total variable cost (fcfa/ha)*	*Total revenue (fcfa/ha)*	*Gross margin (fcfa/ha)*
Mean	143,000	61,000	11,900	21,900	82,300	327,000	394,000	67,000
Median	120,000	59,750	5000	21,000	72,000	280,500	3.90000	84.200
Mode	100,000	70,000	5000	13,500	54,000	355,000	325,000	−300,000
Standard deviation	9.488E4	3.75E4	2.139E4	2.798E4	5.972E4	20.156E4	15.441E4	241,600
Variance	9.00E9	1.40E9	4.57E8	7.82E8	3.56E9	4.06E10	2.38E10	5.837056
Minimum	17,600	5000	0	1500	0	56,400	125,000	−1,000,000
Maximum	800,000	36,000	200,000	250,000	360,000	1,970,000	1,875,000	1,537,600

Source Field Survey, 2014

Correlation Between Technical Efficiency, Profitability and Nutrition Security Status

The policy implications for Nutrition security are presented in Table 9.3. Result shows that technical efficiency estimates and profitability have significant and positive correlation with nutrition security. Specifically, Pearson correlation is negative and significant at 1% level between technical efficiency and nutrition security. This implies that increase in the technical efficiency will increase nutrition security. This could be due to the fact that technical efficiency implies the ability to produce maximum output from a given set of inputs, given the available technology (Aigner et al. 1977). Similarly, Pearson correlation is positive and significant at 1% level between gross margin and nutrition security. This implies that increase in profitability will increase nutrition security. This may be explained by the fact that increment in the profitability is likely to increase rice farmers' income which will enable them to purchase more foodstuffs. Furthermore, Pearson correlation is positive and significant at 1% level between profitability and technical efficiency. This implies that increase in technical efficiency will increase profitability. This could be due to the fact that technical efficiency optimizes resources use in production which may also increase their profitability (Table 9.5).

Table 9.5 Policy implications for nutrition security

		Nutrition security	*Technical efficiency*	*Profitability*
Nutrition security	Pearson correlation	1	0.665**	0.754**
	Sig. (2-tailed)		0.000	0.000
	N	192	192	192
Technical efficiency	Pearson correlation	0.665**	1	0.590**
	Sig. (2-tailed)	0.000		0.000
	N	192	192	192
Profitability	Pearson correlation	0.754**	0.590**	1
	Sig. (2-tailed)	0.000	0.000	
	N	192	192	192

Note **Correlation is significant at the 0.01 level (2-tailed)
Source Author's creation

Conclusion and Recommendations

This study was carried out to analyze productivity among smallholder rice farmers and its policy implications for nutrition security in the West Region of Cameroon. The results show that small scale rice farmers are relatively productive. Further, an increase in technical efficiency and profitability will increase the nutrition security among smallholder rice farmers in the study area. The following are recommended based on the aforementioned conclusion:

(i) Since the study revealed that most small scale farmers are productive, government should develop a strategy that focuses on ways of attracting and encouraging smallholder farmers to embark into rice production.
(ii) Ministry of Agriculture and Rural Development through extension officers should frequently organize training and monitoring aimed at inputs utilization which will increase small scale farmers' output in the study area.
(iii) Government should aim to improve farmers' profit margin through inputs subsidies which will increase both income and output and thereby increase their nutrition security.

References

ACDIC (Association for the Defence of Collective Interests). (2006). *Food Sovereignty in Cameroon: A Study Based on the Rice Sector* (p. 150). Cameroon: Yaoundé.

Ahmadu, J., & Erhabor, P. O. (2012). Determinants of Technical Efficiency of Rice Farmers in Taraba State, Nigeria. *Nigerian Journal of Agriculture, Food and Environment, 8*(3), 78–84.

Aigner, D. C., Knox, L., & Schmidt, P. (1977). Formulation and Estimation of Stochastic Frontier Production Function Models. *Journal of Econometrics, 6*, 21–37.

Amadou, N. (2007, January). *Analysis of Factors Affecting the Technical Efficiency of Arabica Coffee Producers in Cameroon* (AERC Research paper 163, African Economic Research Consortium). Nairobi, pp. 1–51.

Bamou, E., & Masters, W. A. (2007). *Distortions to Agricultural Incentives in Cameroon* (Agricultural Distortion Working Paper 4). World Bank Development Research Group, p. 6.

Bime, M. J., Fouda, T. M., & Mai-Bong, J. T. (2014). Analysis of the Profitability and Marketing Channels of Rice: A Case Study of Menchum River Valley, North-West Region, Cameroon. *Asian Journal of Agriculture and Rural Development, 4*(6), 352–360.

Binam, J. N., Tonye, J., & Njankoua, W. (2005). Source of Technical Efficiency Among Smallholder Farmers in the Slash and Burn Agriculture Zone of Cameroon. *Journal of Economic Cooperation, 26*(1), 193–210.

Dimelu, M. U., Okoye, B. C., Agwu, A. E., Aniedu, O. C., & Akinpela, A. O. (2009). Determinants of Gender Efficiency of Smallholder Cocoyam Farmers in Nsukka Agriculture Zone of Enugu State. *Scientific Research and Essay. Academic Journals, 4*(1), 28–30.

Djomo, C. R. F. (2015). *Analysis of Technical Efficiency and Profitability in Small Scale Rice Production in the West Region of Cameroon* (Thesis Submitted to the Department of Agricultural Economics). University of Agriculture, Makurdi in partial fulfilment of the requirements for the award of Master of Science in Agricultural Economics, 72 p.

Dontsop, P. M., Rhaji, A. Y., & Adelakun, O. J. (2009). Determinants of Technical Efficiency of Cocoa Farmers in Cameroon: The Case Study of Central Province. *Journal of Economics and Social Studies, 6*, 32–53.

Food and Agriculture Organization of the United Nations (FAO). (2006). Brief on Import Surges, Countries, n°4, Cameroon: Poultry, Rice and Vegetable Oils. Commodities and Trade Division, Rome, Italy, p. 20.

Fonjong, L., & Mbah, F. A. (2007). The Fortunes and Misfortunes of Women Rice Producers in Ndop-Cameroon: The Implications for Gender Roles. *Journal of International Women's Studies, 8*(4), 133–134.

Gama, E. (2013). *Analysis of Productivity and Economic Efficiency of Cocoa Farmers in the South-West Region of Cameroon* (PhD thesis submitted at the Department of Agricultural Economics and Rural Sociology). Faculty of Agriculture, Ahmadu Bello University, Zaria, Nigeria, 1 p.

Gbetnkom, D., & Khan, S. A. (2002). *Determinants of Agricultural Exports: The Case of Cameroon Being an Emerging Country* (An African Economic Research Consortium Research Paper 120), Nairobi, Kenya.

Idiong, C. I., Agom, D. I., & Ohen, S. B. (2006). Comparative Analysis of Technical Efficiency in Swamp Rice and Upland Rice Production Systems in Cross River State Nigeria. In *Proceedings of Farm Management Association of Nigeria from 18–21 September.*

INS (Institut National de la Statistique). (2005). Les Comptes Nationaux du Cameroun. Yaoundé, 200 p.

Ministry of Agriculture and Rural Development, (2009). *National Strategy for Rice Growing in Cameroon (Milling III).* p. 7. Retrieved from https://www.jica.go.jp/english/our_work/thematic_issues/agricultural/pdf/cameroon_en.pdf.

Ministère de l'Agriculture et du développement Rural (MINADER). (2008). *Statistique Agricole du Cameroun 008, Campagne 2008/200*, Yaoundé, Cameroun, pp. 33–34.

Ministère de l'Agriculture (MINAGRI). (2002). *Statistique Agricole du Cameroun 009, Campagne 2001/2002*, Yaoundé, Cameroun, p. 45.

Molua, E. L. (2010). Response of Rice Yields in Cameroon: Some Implications for Agricultural Price Policy. *Libyan Agriculture Research Center Journal Internation, 1*(2), 182–194.

Piebeb, G. (2008). Evaluating the Constraints and Opportunity for Sustainable Rice Production in Cameroon. *Research Journal of Agriculture and Biological Sciences, 4*(6), 734–744.

Simonyan, J. B., Umoren, B. D., & Okoye, B. C. (2011). Gender Differentials in Technical Efficiency Among Maize Farmers in Essien Udim Local Government Area, Nigeria. *International Journal of Economics and Management Sciences, 2*(1), 17–23.

Umeh, J. C., & Ataborh, E. M. (2011). *Efficiency of Rice Farmers in Nigeria: Potentials for Food Security and Poverty Alleviation*. IFMA 16—Theme 3, pp. 1–13.

World Bank. (2007). *Cameroon at Glance*. Retrieved on June 28, 2014 from http://devdata.worldbank.org/AAG/cmr_aag.pdf.

World factsbook. (2010). *Cameroon Economy*. Retrieved on November 10, 2015 from www.cia.gov/cia/publication/factsbook/goes/htm.

Yerima, B. P. K., & Van, R. E. (2005). *Soils of Cameroon, Distribution, Genesis, Characteristics, Management and Utilization* (pp. 52–54). Yaoundé: Edition clef.

CHAPTER 10

Maximizing Agricultural Growth Policy Space Through Public Expenditures and Foreign Direct Investment in Cameroon (1985–2016)

Djomo Choumbou Raoul Fani, Aye Goodness Chioma, Ukpe Udeme Henrietta, Ngo Valery Ngo, Gbadebo Odularu, and Oben Njock Emmanuel

D. C. R. Fani (✉)
Faculty of Agriculture and Veterinary Medicine, Department of Agricultural Economics and Agribusiness, University of Buea, Buea, Cameroon

A. G. Chioma
Department of Agricultural Economics, University of Agriculture, Makurdi, Nigeria

U. U. Henrietta
Department of Agricultural Economics and Extension, Federal University Wukari, Wukari, Nigeria

N. V. Ngo
Section for Social Medicine and Epidemiology, Department of Global Health, The Sahlgrenska Academy, University of Gothenburg, Gothenburg, Sweden

G. Odularu
Department of Economics and Finance, Bay Atlantic University, Washington, DC, USA

O. N. Emmanuel
Department of Agricultural Economics and Agribusiness, University of Buea, Buea, Cameroon

G. Odularu (ed.), *Nutrition, Sustainable Agriculture and Climate Change in Africa*,
https://doi.org/10.1007/978-3-030-47875-9_10

Introduction

Prior to the economic crisis in the 1980s, Cameroon enjoyed steady economic growth and relative social stability for about 20 years following independence in 1960. The average annual growth rate of Gross Domestic Product (GDP) hovered around 5% which was driven mainly by the agricultural sector (Benjamin and Devarajan 1986; Essama-Nssah and Bassolé 2010). The country's agricultural sector plays an essential role in the economy and needs to extend its contribution to growth and combating poverty. It currently accounts for 21.7% of GDP and involves 70% of the active population (World Bank 2013). It plays a determining role in the war on poverty and food insecurity, thanks to the self-provisioning of 2,000,000 agricultural households in the country and in the supply of food products to neighbourhood and urban markets. It is estimated that some 80% of the food requirements of the country's population is satisfied by domestic production (World Bank 2013).

Public expenditure is an aspect of fiscal policy which is widely seen as stabilization tool and hence, plays a very crucial role in stimulating growth. As a wing of the government budget, public expenditure has stimulated large empirical debates on its impact on growth (Ahmed and Mubarak 2014). The role of the government in economic management is performed through the formulation and implementation of economic policy generally and fiscal policy in particular. As recognized by the new growth theory, public expenditure is an important factor for self-sustaining productivity gains and long-term growth. For instance, government expenditures may contribute to agricultural growth (and hence poverty alleviation), it may indirectly create rural nonfarm jobs and increased wages. The real significance of government expenditures lies in the fact that it imparts a greater amount of "trickle-down" benefits for the poor in the growth process than growth alone (Fan et al. 2000; Van de Walle 1996; Galal 2003; Elijah 2011).

Private capital and investment climate are central drivers to achieving and regenerating strong, sustainable and balanced economic growth in the developing world. The main challenge for developing countries over the years was to provide, sustain and enable business environment for domestic and foreign investments. Foreign aids, public and private capitals used by the governmental and the private sectors are still in debate since the strategy of great investments called big push (Tchouassi 2014). Faced with economic crisis, Cameroon resorted to the lobbying and encouragement of foreign aids, foreign investment and export-oriented production as panacea for sustainable economic growth that could be trickled down to poverty reduction. Many macroeconomic measures and institutional reforms became fashionable and with the assistance of the World Bank, the Structural Adjustment Programme (SAP) was adopted and ushered into the economic growth and sustainable development agendas of Cameroon (Abit 2014). Some progress appeared to have been made when the average annual foreign direct investment (FDI) inflow into Cameroon increased from \$284 million and \$270 million in 2007 and 2008, respectively, to \$337 million in 2009, primarily because of higher oil prices (Efiong 2013).

Since 1960, government spending has been the major instrument to reduce poverty in Cameroon. Also, private investment is desirable as it may help to stimulate growth in the economy which is necessary to generate resources required for future spending. Sustainable agricultural progress is an adequate means of providing a permanent solution to poverty traps and increasing the overall welfare of mankind. Keynesian theory assumes that public expenditures culminate into economic activities that lead to growth in the economy and by implication on the level of poverty. On the other hand, classical economists are of the view that increasing government expenditures does not necessarily increase the national output; instead, they assert that higher government expenditures slow down the overall performance of the economy. For instance, in an attempt to finance the rising expenditure, government may increase taxes and/or borrowing. Thus, higher taxes reduce income and aggregate demand. In the same vein, higher profit tax tends to increase production costs and reduce investment expenditures as well as profitability of firms (Ghali 1998; Vedder and Gallaway 1998). Following the attainment of the decision point of the enhanced initiative for heavily indebted poor countries initiative (HIPC), the government of Cameroon drew up successively a second-generation poverty reduction strategy paper (PRSP) in 2009 and the growth and employment strategy paper (GESP) in 2010 as a milestone in the process of improving the prosperity of the country by achieving two (2) digits gross domestic product (GDP) by 2035 (IFAD 2012). Although, Cameroon is experienced a dwindling macroeconomic performance with growth averaging 4% and well above the global average of 3% annum (Economic Outlook 2014). However, growing empirical evidence on poverty studies in Cameroon suggests persistence in extreme poverty especially among those living in rural areas and working in agriculture (Fambon et al. 2014; Baye 2010).

Cameroon's public spending increased significantly from 2006 to 2013 period by over 16.6% (Economic Outlook 2014), budgetary constraints have constituted a limited factor in meeting up with international convention. For instance, Food and Agriculture organization (FAO) recommends that government allocates 25% of budgetary provision to agriculture; the 2003 Maputo declaration recommended 10% of budgetary provision should be allocated to agriculture by government. These stipulated percentages have never been respected by the government of Cameroon, thereby affecting the performance of the agricultural sector as well as the poverty profile of the country. In an attempt to facilitate economic growth and development, the government of Cameroon has enacted several laws and decrees to encourage foreign capital inflows prior to the advent of the Structural Adjustment Programme (SAP), but poor growth still prevails (Forgha 2008).

Public expenditures and foreign investment are macroeconomic instruments used for stability in developing economy like Cameroon. Given this position, this study will provide reliable information for future projection which will enable the Ministry of Economic and Planning to make crucial decision regarding current situation. In addition, it will also enable us to know whether the country is adequately managing its resources and investing it wisely.

The effects of public expenditures and foreign direct investment on agricultural growth will be used as a benchmark to assess the degree to which public expenditures, agricultural growth and foreign direct investment are mutually dependent on each other. It will help the government to know whether they have negative, neutral or positive relationships over time. The present study will also extend understanding on the relationships between government expenditures, agricultural sector growth and private investment by employing updated data. In addition, the investigation of such relationships will also be useful in the sense that it will promote a greater understanding of the implications for poverty alleviation in Cameroon.

Analysis of the sensitivity of agricultural growth to increases/decreases in public expenditures and foreign direct investment will give more insight on the extent to which policies adjustment can be done in order to sustain the agricultural sector by increasing/reducing public expenditures or encouraging/discouraging private investment and these will enable the ministry of planning to develop a strategy on whether to encourage both private investment and public expenditure. It will also bring to the fore the degree to which changes in public expenditures and foreign direct investment can influence agricultural growth.

This study will also provide critical economic information on the future outcome based upon the past result which will help to validate or invalidate the theory increasing, stagnating or decreasing of both public expenditures and private investment. The study will further provide the most efficient way of spending public resources as well as setting policy to enhance private investment in the economy over time in order to sustain the growth of agriculture. Given the conflicting views between Keynesians and Neoclassical economists on the relationships between public expenditures, growth and private investment in the economy, it is,therefore, important to carry out this research in the context of Cameroon.

Several studies have been carried out on public expenditures, private investment and economic growth with little or no emphasis on the response of agricultural growth to public expenditure and foreign direct investment. For instance, Tabi et al. (2009) assessed who benefits from combined Tax and public expenditure policies in Cameroon; National Institute of Statistics (NIS) (2009) conducted second survey on the monitoring of public expenditures and the level of receipts satisfaction in the education and health in Cameroon; Foueka (2011) attempted to justify the growth of public expenditures in Cameroon; World bank (2013) reviewed basic agricultural public expenditures diagnostic from 2003–2012 in Cameroon; Efiong (2013) analyzed foreign direct investments in developing African Countries: Their effects on the economic growth in Cameroon (2006–2011); Fambon (2013) examined the impact of foreign capital inflows (which include foreign aid and foreign direct investment) on economic growth in Cameroon; Kum (2009) carried out a study on foreign direct investment in Cameroon; Forgha (2008) examined the link between foreign direct investment and economic performance in Cameroon. This study fills the gap in the literature by analyzing how to maximize agricultural growth policy space through public expenditures and foreign direct investment in Cameroon.

Literature Review

Conceptual Framework

The response of agricultural growth to public expenditures and foreign direct investment in Cameroon (Fig. 10.1) is conceptualized in terms of inflow, stock variables, outflow and policy variables (public expenditures and foreign direct investment). Inflow increases stock variables while outflow decreases stock variables. For instance, employment rate increases the workforce while death/firing reduces the workforce. Domestic credit to the private sector increases gross domestic private investment while depreciation decreases gross domestic private investment. Rate of taxes increases government revenue while subsidy reduces government revenue. Agricultural production increases food supply while consumption decreases food supply. Increases in food supply increases government revenue through taxes paid by investors in the food supply chain and reduces subsidies given by government. Increases in food supply

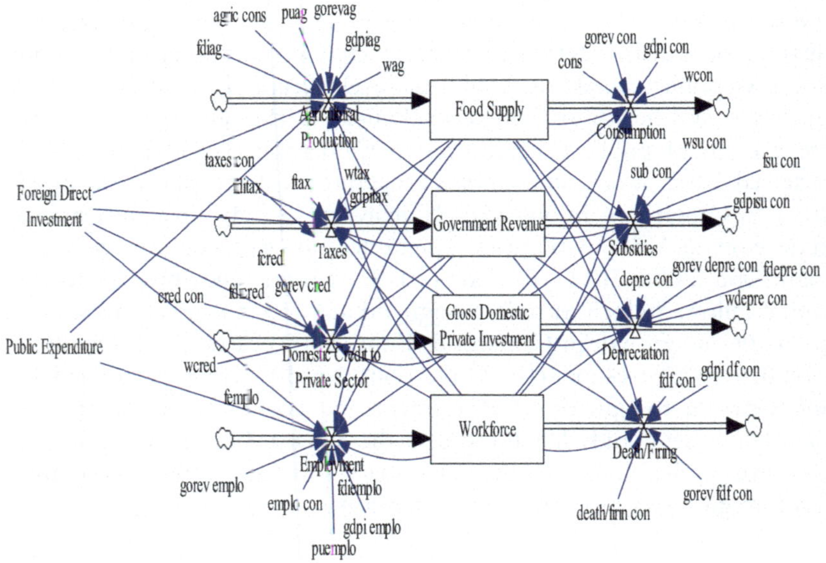

Fig. 10.1 Conceptual Framework for response of agricultural growth to public expenditures and foreign direct investment in Cameroon: 1985–2016 (*Source* Adapted from Sukhdev et al. [2015])

also increases investment in the food chain through demand for credit while decreases in food supply affect gross domestic private investment. Increases in food supply also increases employment in the food supply chain while decreases in food supply increases death/firing of workers in the food supply chain. Government revenue determines the level of public expenditure. For instance, government purchases the services of households, makes transfer payments in form of old ages pensions, unemployment relief, sickness benefit, etc., and also spend on them through allocation in various sector of the economy such as agriculture, health, education, roads and targeted programmes (Jhingan 2010). The indirect effect of public expenditure comes from higher agricultural wages and improved nonfarm employment opportunities induced by growth in the agricultural sector. Public expenditure on education, for instance, promotes labour, human and physical capital for agriculture, as well as public expenditure on health, promotes access to primary health care to farmers. In addition, public expenditure on roads enable transfers of agricultural produces from rural to urban areas as well as public expenditure on targeted programme increases farmer's efficiency (Fan 2007). Similarly government purchases all its requirement of goods of all types from private investor, gives subsidies and makes transfer payments to firms in order to encourage production (Jhingan 2010). Foreign direct investment and gross domestic private investment affect indirectly agricultural growth through infrastructural development, financial sector development, human resources, research and innovation, targeted programmes. Moreover, it also affects agricultural production directly through investment on farmhouses, orchards, plantations, farm employment, land acquisition and building. Foreign direct investment increases government revenue through the payment of taxes by foreign investors. It also affects gross domestic private investment through their technical expertise and huge capital as well as the use of domestic credit that may lead to reduce the competitiveness of domestic investors. Workforce affects agricultural production through the supply of manpower. It also affects consumption through purchase of goods and services by workers. It increases government revenue through income tax. It also increases domestic investment through use of credit by workers, the rate of tax subsidies increases household consumption of workers while death/firing decreases consumption and gross domestic private investment.

where:

agric cons is the rate at which agricultural production affect food supply

gdpiag is the rate at which gross domestic private investment affect agricultural production

fdiag is the rate at which foreign direct investment affect agricultural production

puag is the rate at which public expenditure affect agricultural production

goverag is the rate at which government revenue affect agricultural production

wag is the rate at which workforce affect agricultural production

taxes con is the rate at which taxes affect government revenue

gdpitax is the rate at which gross domestic private investment affect taxes

ftax is the rate at which food supply affect taxes

wtax is the rate at which workforce affect taxes

fditax is the rate at which foreign direct investment affect taxes

cred con is the rate at which domestic credit to private sector affect gross domestic private investment

fdicred is the rate at which foreign direct investment affect domestic credit to private sector

fcred is the rate at which food supply affect domestic credit to private sector

govercred is the rate at which government revenue affect domestic credit to private sector

wcred is the rate at which workforce affect domestic credit to private sector

emplo con is the rate at which employment affect workforce

gdpiemplo is the rate at which gross domestic private investment affect employment

fdiemplo is the rate at which foreign direct investment affect employment

femplo is the rate at which food supply affect employment

goveremplo is the rate at which government revenue affect employment

puexpemplo is the rate at which public expenditure affect employment

cons is the rate at which consumption affect food supply

gorevcon is the rate at which government revenue affect consumption

wcon is the rate at which workforce affect consumption

gdpicon is the rate at which gross domestic private investment affect consumption

sub con is the rate at which subsidies affect government revenue

gdpisu con is the rate at which gross domestic private investment affect subsidies

fsu con is the rate at which food supply affect subsidies

wsu con is the rate at which workforce affect subsidies

depre con is the rate at which depreciation affect gross domestic private investment

goverdepre con is the rate at which government revenue affect depreciation

wdepre con is the rate at which workforce affect depreciation

fdepre con is the rate at which food supply affect depreciation

death/firing con is the rate at which death/firing affect workforce

gdpidfcon is the rate at which gross domestic private investment affect death/firing

fdfcon is the rate at which food supply affect death/firing

goverfdf con is the rate at which government revenue affect death/firing.

Empirical Review on Simulation/Sensitivity Studies

Gelauff and Lejour (2006) used general equilibrium (GE) model to provide *ex ante* estimates of the impact on labour productivity and GDP growth of achieving the European Union's target reduction in administrative burdens. They found that 25% reduction in administrative costs on average labour productivity and economic growth in the European Union will rise by 1.5 and 0.9%, respectively, by 2025.

The Central Planning Bureau (CPB) of the Netherlands Bureau for Economic Policy Analysis (2004) used general equilibrium (GE) model to estimate the reduction of administrative burdens for businesses within the European Union and found that the initial impact on GDP from reducing administrative costs by 25% was around 1.1%. The longer-term effect was even larger, with an increase in real GDP of 1.4% attributed to higher savings, more investment and extra capital. When allowance is made, the long-term effect on real GDP is 1.7% for the European Union.

Vaqar et al. (2013) used a dynamic computable general equilibrium model linked with microsimulation model to estimate the macro-micro impact of public infrastructure investment in Pakistan. Two approaches to public investment were considered in their simulations. In the first, production taxes finance the additional public infrastructure investment and in the second, foreign borrowing provides resources. Their results revealed that public infrastructure investments have the same direction of impact whether funded by taxation or international borrowing, particularly when looking at macroeconomic gains and poverty reduction in the long run. However, in the very short run, tax financing puts a strain on output in the industrial sector and thus reduces economic growth in the short run. The financing from international borrowing has a Dutch disease-like impact in the short run.

Rioja (2001) used computable general equilibrium model on Brazil, Mexico and Peru and showed that these countries underinvested in infrastructure during 1970s and 1980s. The simulations suggest that infrastructure can positively impact output, private investment and welfare.

Estache et al. (2009) used computable general equilibrium model to show that foreign aid-funded infrastructure does produce Dutch Disease effects, but that the negative impacts differ by the type of investment. Economic growth attenuates these negative effects.

Dissou and Didic (2011) used computable general equilibrium model to indicate that the crowding-out effects of public infrastructure is sensitive to the mode of financing chosen by the government. Overall, their findings suggest that public investment in infrastructure can support private investment and sustain capital accumulation. The positive impact of public investment on private investment can be explained through the infrastructure financing channels such as public-private partnerships and subcontracting which in turn tend to crowd-in private investment.

Wautabouna (2012) used micro simulated general equilibrium approach to analyze public expenditure contribution to pro-poor growth in Ivory Coast. He found that the Ivorian authorities contributed meaningfully to poverty reduction. In other words, the poor benefited from the fruits of the economic growth induced by public investments.

Władysław (2010) used a long-term simulation model for Poland's economy and found that Poland may have a chance to reach the average level of the European Union (15) countries in 2030 only in the optimistic scenario, while in the pessimistic scenario it would remain at the 46% level.

Most of these empirical literatures reviewed focused on the effect of changes of exogenous variables with no emphasis on the system dynamic approach using differential equations. Hence there is a need to carry this study to empirically document and fills the knowledge gap.

Methodology

The Study Area: The study was conducted in Cameroon which has ten regions, namely: Centre; Littoral; Adamawa; Far-North; North; South; East; West; North-West and South-West. The country covers a total land area of 475,442 sq km and is located in the Central part of Africa within latitudes 2° and 13° North and longitude 9° and 16° East of the equator (United Nations, 2004). Cameroon is bordered by Nigeria to the West; Chad to the Northeast; the Central Africa Republic to the East and Equatorial Guinea, Gabon and Republic of Congo to the South (World factsbook 2010).

Cameroon's natural resources are very well suited to agriculture and arboriculture. An estimated 70% of the population farms and agriculture comprised an estimated 19.8% of GDP in 2009 (Delancy and Delancy 2000). The agricultural sector is dominated by small scale farmers who use manual tools. They sell their surplus produce and some maintain separate fields for commercial use. Urban areas are particularly reliant on small scale producers for their foodstuffs. Soils and climate on the coast encourage extensive commercial cultivation of bananas, cocoa, oil palms, rubber and tea. Inland on the South Cameroon Plateau, cash crops include coffee, sugar and tobacco (Delancy and Delancy 2000). Coffee is a major cash crop in the western highlands and in the north, natural conditions favour crops such as cotton, groundnuts and rice. Reliance on agricultural exports makes Cameroon vulnerable to shifts in their prices (Delancy and Delancy 2000). Livestock is raised throughout the country and fishing employs about 5000 people and provides over 100,000 tons of seafood each year (Som 2013). Bushmeat, long a staple food for rural Cameroonians, is today a delicacy in the country's urban centres. The commercial bushmeat trade has now surpassed deforestation as the main threat to wildlife in Cameroon (Delancy and Delancy 2000). The southern rainforest has vast timber reserves, estimated to cover 37% of Cameroon's total land area (Delancy and Delancy 2000).

Method of Data Collection: Due to the unavailability of data, annual time series covering a period of 32 years (1985–2016) were obtained from the World Bank development indicators data base, Ministry of economic and planning. Food and Agriculture organization (FAO), world atlas database and united nations conference on trade and development (UNCTAD).

Techniques of Data Analysis: Ordinary differential equation (ODEs) was used to analyze the broad objective involving three (3) scenarios

Model Specification

Ordinary Differential Equation

The model was specified as follows

Minimizing

$$\varepsilon_{1985}^{2016} = \varepsilon(Y_{\text{data}} - \text{Agric}) \tag{10.1}$$

where:

$\varepsilon_{1985}^{2016}$ is a defined function

Y_{data} is historical data

Agric is the simulated data

$$\frac{\text{dAgric}}{\text{dt}} = \beta_1\text{fds} + \beta_2\text{fdi} + \beta_3\text{puexp} + \beta_4\text{gorev} + \beta_5\text{gdpi} + \beta_6\text{workf} \tag{10.2}$$

$$\frac{\text{dfds}}{\text{dt}} = \text{fdso} + \int_{1985}^{2016} (\text{Agric} - \text{Consumption}) \tag{10.3}$$

$$\frac{\text{dgorev}}{\text{dt}} = \text{gorevo} + \int_{1985}^{2016} (\text{taxes} - \text{subsidy}) \tag{10.4}$$

$$\frac{\text{dgdpi}}{\text{dt}} = \text{gdpio} + \int_{1985}^{2016} (\text{credit to private sector} - \text{depreciation}) \tag{10.5}$$

$$\frac{\text{dworkf}}{\text{dt}} = \text{workfo} + \int_{1985}^{2016} (\text{employment} - \text{death/firing}) \tag{10.6}$$

where:

$$\frac{\text{dconsumption}}{\text{dt}} = \beta_5\text{fd} + \beta_6\text{gorev} + \beta_7\text{gdpi} + \beta_8\text{workf} \tag{10.7}$$

$$\frac{\text{dtaxes}}{\text{dt}} = \beta_9\text{fds} + \beta_{10}\text{fdi} + \beta_{11}\text{gorev} + \beta_{12}\text{gdpi} + \beta_{13}\text{workf} \tag{10.8}$$

$$\frac{\text{dsubsidy}}{\text{dt}} = \beta_{14}\text{fds} + \beta_{15}\text{gorev} + \beta_{16}\text{gdpi} + \beta_{17}\text{workf} \tag{10.9}$$

$$\frac{\text{dcredit to private sector}}{\text{dt}} = \beta_{18}\text{fds} + \beta_{19}\text{fdi} + \beta_{20}\text{gorev} + \beta_{21}\text{gdpi} + \beta_{22}\text{workf} \tag{10.10}$$

$$\frac{\text{ddepreciation}}{\text{dt}} = \beta_{23}\text{fds} + \beta_{24}\text{gorev} + \beta_{25}\text{gdpi} + \beta_{26}\text{workf} \tag{10.11}$$

$$\frac{\text{demployment}}{\text{dt}} = \beta_{27}\text{fds} + \beta_{28}\text{fdi} + \beta_{29}\text{puexp} + \beta_{30}\text{gorev} + \beta_{31}\text{gdpi} + \beta_{32}\text{workf} \tag{10.12}$$

$$\frac{\text{ddeath/firing}}{\text{dt}} = \beta_{33}\text{fds} + \beta_{34}\text{gorev} + \beta_{35}\text{gdpi} + \beta_{36}\text{workf} \tag{10.13}$$

agricultural growth (agric) is measured in tons
food supply (fds) is measured in tons
government revenue (gorev) is measured in cfa
gross domestic private investment (gdpi) is measured in cfa
workforce (workf) is measured per thousands
foreign direct investment (fdi) is measured in cfa
public expenditures (puexp) is measured in cfa
taxes is measured in cfa
subsidy is measured in cfa
domestic credit to private sector is measured in cfa
depreciation is measured in percentage
employment is measured per thousands
death/firing is measured per thousands
fdso is the initial value of food supply
gorevo is the initial value of government revenue
gdpio is the initial value of gross domestic private investment
workfo is the initial value of workforce.

Sensitivity Analysis of Agricultural Growth to Increases/Decreases in Public Expenditures and Foreign Direct Investment

By differentiating Eq. (10.2) with respect to public expenditures and foreign direct investment, the differential equation for the sensitivity of agricultural growth is defined as follows:

$$\nabla S_{AG}(t, P) = \frac{d_{Agric}}{dfdi} + \frac{dAgric}{dpuexp} \tag{10.14}$$

where:

∇S_{AG} = changes in agricultural growth (in tons)
foreign direct investment (fdi) is measured in cfa
public expenditure (puexp)is measured in cfa
t = period
P = parameters

Results and Discussion

Model Validation

The result of test of difference between the original and the baseline simulated data in Table 10.1 shows that t-value (−0.53) was not significant indicating that there is no significant difference between the simulated baseline data and original data. Therefore, the simulated baseline data is fitted to carry out the study (Fig. 10.2).

Sensitivity of Agricultural Growth to Increase in Foreign Direct Investment and Decrease in Public Expenditures by 15% (Scenario 1)

The sensitivity of agricultural growth to increase in foreign direct investment and decrease in public expenditures by 15% is shown in Fig. 10.3 while Table 10.2 presents the summary statistics. The results in Table 10.2 show that the simulated data (scenario1) ranges from 114.43 tons to 1.78E+27 tons with average of 15,906,600,725.58

Table 10.1 Test of difference between the original and the baseline simulated data

	T	*df*	*Significance (2—tailed)*	*Decision rule*
Equal variances assumed	−0.53	62	0.59	Accept Ho
Equal variances not assumed	−0.53	38.31	0.59	

Source Author's creation

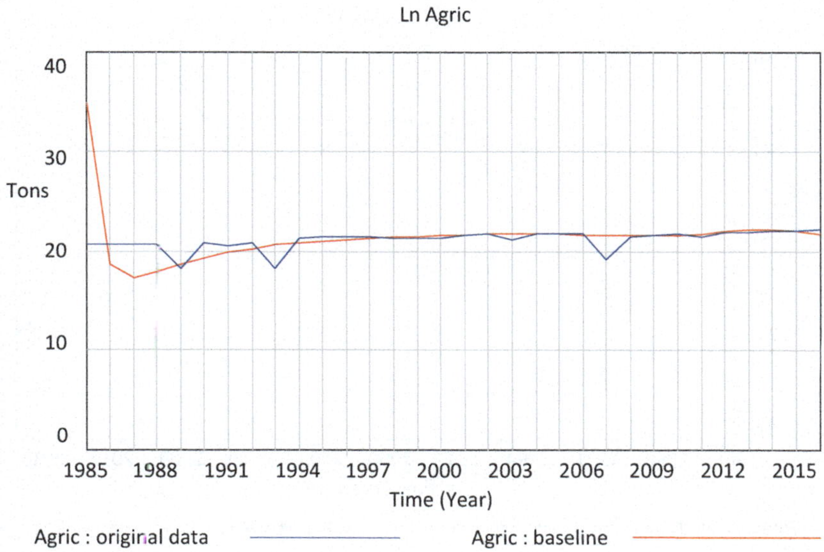

Fig. 10.2 Model structure fitness (*Source* Author's creation)

tons compared to the baseline which ranges from 31,960,138.10 tons to 1,470,000,000,000,000 tons with average of 1,967,441,884 tons. This result could be attributed to the fact that foreign investors come with huge capital and technical expertise which may lead to increase in the growth of agriculture. This result agrees with Fambon (2013) who found that foreign direct investment inflow increased the economic growth of Cameroon. Specifically, from 1985 to 1991, the simulated data (scenario 1) was below the baseline from 981,398,783,472,675 to 374,087,393.29 tons compared to 1,470,000,000,000,000 tons to 426,021,341.33 tons for baseline. This could be due to the low rate of foreign direct investment inflow during the period. From 1992 to 1996, the simulated data (scenario 1) rose slightly above the simulated baseline data from 1,112,638,434.75 tons to 5,138,361,030.99 tons compared to 648,388,103.4 tons to 1,578,909,096.08 tons for baseline. From 1997 to 2002, the simulated data (scenario 1) decreased below the simulated baseline from 1,693,392,923 tons to 3,024,464,838.84 tons compared to 1,744,964,415.27 tons to 247,622,2375.16 tons for baseline. From 2003 to 2007, the simulated data (scenario 1) rose above the

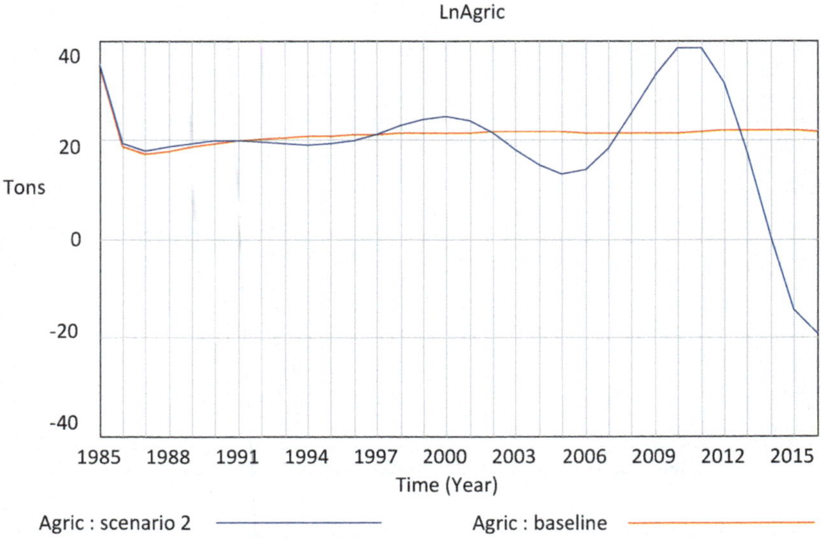

Fig. 10.3 Sensitivity of agricultural growth to decrease in foreign direct investment and increase in public expenditures by 15% (*Source* Author's creation)

Table 10.2 Summary statistics for the simulated scenario 1 and baseline agricultural growth

	Scenario 1	*Baseline*
Mean	15,906,600,725.58	1,967,441,884
Minimum	114.43	31,960,138.10
Maximum	1.78E+27	1,470,000,000,000,000

Source Author's creation

simulated baseline from 8, 883,0864,521.92 tons to 49,736,255,946.41 tons compared to 2,682,459,675.70 tons to 2,577,278,927.36 tons for baseline. This could be attributed to the full implementation of projects set up by foreign investors. This result agrees with the findings of Uboh et al. (2012) who found that increased private investment increased the agricultural growth in Nigeria. From 2008 to 2012, the simulated data (scenario 1) decreased slightly below the baseline from 36,397,112.40 tons to 237,993.82 tons compared to 2,379,128,307.05

tons to 2,905,873,876.25 tons for baseline. This may be attributed to the world economic crisis which must have reduced businesses in the country. From 2013 to 2016, the simulated data (scenario 1) rose slightly above the baseline as it ranges from 52,379,128,307.05 tons to 1.78E+27 tons compared to 4,291,919,904.66 tons to 2,994,370,910.87 tons for the baseline. This could still be attributed to the full implementation of investment set by foreign investors. This result agrees with the findings of Uboh et al. (2012) who found that increased private investment increases the agricultural growth in Nigeria.

Sensitivity of Agricultural Growth to Decrease in Foreign Direct Investment and Increase in Public Expenditures by 15% (Scenario 2)
The sensitivity of agricultural growth to decrease in foreign direct investment and increase in public expenditures by 15% is shown in Fig. 10.4 while Table 10.3 presents the summary. Results showed that the simulated data (scenario 2) ranges from 5.01E-09 tons to 61,634,612,568,897,700 with average of 248,263,192.13 tons compared to the baseline which

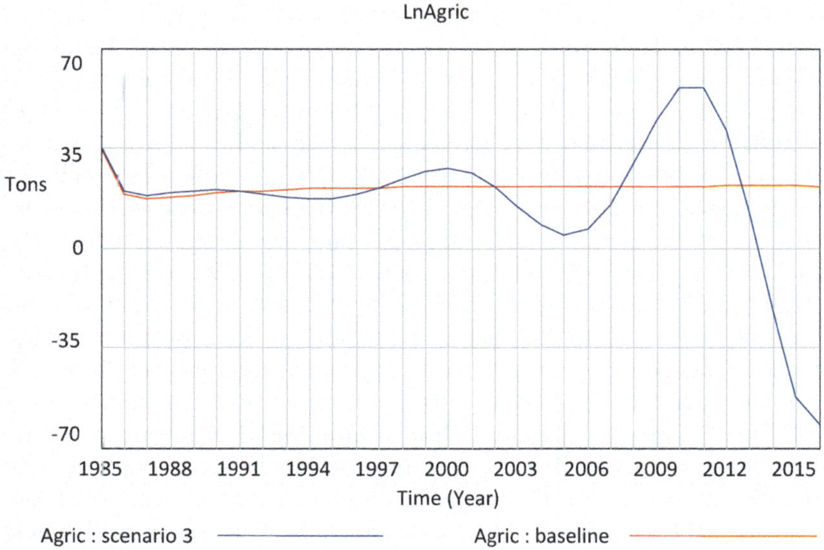

Fig. 10.4 Sensitivity of agricultural growth to increases in foreign direct investment and public expenditures by 15% (*Source* Author's creation)

Table 10.3 Summary statistics for the simulated scenario 2 and baseline agricultural growth

	Scenario 2	*Baseline*
Mean	248,263,192.13	1,967,441,884
Minimum	5.01E-09	31,960,138.10
Maximum	61,634,612,568,897,700	1,470,000,000,000,000

Source Author's creation

ranges from 31,960,138.10 to 1,470,000,000,000,000 tons with average of 1,967,441,884 tons. This result may be attributed to the fact that increase in public expenditures is generally associated with increases in taxes which in turn reduces foreign direct investment, therefore reduces the growth of the agricultural sector. This result agrees with Belinga et al. (2017) who found that increase in government expenditures decreases the economic growth of Cameroon in the long run. Specifically, from 1985 to 1991, the simulated data (scenario 2) rose slightly above the baseline from 225,066,022,1810,350 tons to 485,165,195.40 tons compared to 1,478,789,141,224,740 tons to 426,021,341.33 tons for baseline. From 1992 to 1996, the simulated data (scenario 2) decreased below the baseline from 374,087,393.3 tons to 480,337,721.1 tons compared to 648,388,103.4 tons to 1,578,909,096.08 tons for baseline. From 1997 to 2001, the simulated data (scenario 2) rose slightly above the baseline from 1,798,106,493.3 tons to 23,493,743,767.65 tons compared to 2,935,078,394.23 tons to 2,263,096,850.33 tons for baseline. From 2002 to 2007, the simulated data (scenario 2) decreased below the baseline from 2,355,455,584.86 tons to 113,805,339.7 tons compared to 2,476,222,375.16 tons to 2,577,278,927.36 tons for baseline. This could be attributed to the fact that investment done by both foreign investors and government invested in capital expenditures which do not necessarily produce expected results in the short run. This result agrees with the findings of Ibrahim (2000) who found that public investment is unproductive, because the relationship between public capital formation and the growth rate of income per capita is negative. From 2008 to 2012, the simulated data (scenario 2) rose above the baseline from 112,926,161,045.81 tons to 53,462,415,022,408.8 tons compared to 2,379,128,307.05 tons to 1,762,501,599.20 tons for baseline. This result agrees with the findings of Uboh et al. (2012) who found that increase in government agricultural spending led to increase in agricultural growth in Nigeria. From 2013 to 2016, the simulated data (scenario 2) decreased below the baseline from 51,649,961.08 tons to 5.01E-09 tons compared to 4,291,919,904.66 tons to 2,994,370,910.87 tons for baseline. This could be due to inadequate monitoring and evaluation of agricultural targeted programmes by government associated with limited foreign investors.

Sensitivity of Agricultural Growth to Increases in Foreign Direct Investment and Public Expenditure by 15% (Scenario 3)

The sensitivity of agricultural growth to increases in foreign direct investment and public expenditures by 15% is shown in Fig. 10.4 while Table 10.4 shows the summary statistics. Results showed that the simulated data (scenario 3) ranges between 2.88E-27 tons to 2.88E+24 tons with average of 28,346,099.64 tons compared to the baseline which ranges from 31,960,138.10 to 1,470,000,000,000,000 tons with average of 1,967,441,884 tons. Focusing on Fig. 10.4, it is observed that from 1985 to 1991, the simulated data (scenario 3) rose slightly above the baseline with values ranging from 3,459,844,358,928,810 to 552,519.895.13 tons compared to 1,478,789,141,224,740 tons to 426,021,341.33 tons for baseline. This may be explained by the complementary policy of increasing both foreign direct investment and public expenditures to sustain the agricultural sector. From 1992 to 1996, the simulated data (scenario 3) were slightly below the baseline from 211,555,937.20 tons to 139,002,155.8 tons compared to 648,388,103.4 tons to 1,578,909,096.08 tons for the baseline. This could be attributed to inconsistency in government policy associated with the slowdown in the activities of foreign investors. From 1997 to 2001, the simulated data (scenario 3) rose slightly above the baseline from 1,852,866,988.55

Table 10.4 Summary statistics for the simulated scenario 7 and baseline agricultural growth

	Scenario 3	*Baseline*
Mean	28,346,099.64	1,967,441,884
Minimum	2.88E-27	31,960,138.10
Maximum	2.88E+24	1,470,000,000,000,000

Source Author's creation

tons to 248,821.099,679.15 tons compared to 2,935,078,394.23 tons to 2,263,096,850.33 tons for baseline. This is attributed to the combined efforts made by government and foreign investors to sustain the agricultural sector. This result agrees with Fatima (2012) who found that the increase in public and private investment had a positive effect on growth. From 2002 to 2007, the simulated data (scenario 3) decreased below the baseline 2,047,734,710.81 tons to 4,685,578.75 tons compared to 2,476,222,375.16 tons to 2,577,278,927.36 tons for baseline. This may be attributed to the slowdown in activities of foreign investors associated with increases in taxes as well as the duplication of agricultural programmes which led to the decline of growth in the agricultural sector. From 2008 to 2012, the simulated data (scenario 3) rose above the baseline from 6,882,478,843,480.97 tons to 1,250,406,034,422,520,000 compared to 2,379,128,307.05 tons to 1,762,501,599.20 tons for baseline. This could be attributed to the complementary policy set up to sustain the growth of the agricultural sector. From 2013 to 2016, the simulated data (scenario 3) decreased below the baseline from 660,003.22 tons to 2.88E-27 tons compared to 4,291,919,904.66 tons to 2,994,370,910.87 tons for baseline. This could be attributed to a lack of adequate planning to sustain the agricultural sector.

Conclusion and Recommendations

This study analyzed how to maximize agricultural growth policy space through public expenditures and foreign direct investment in Cameroon from 1985 to 2016. The study further showed that increase in foreign direct investment and decrease in public expenditures (scenario 1) provided the best alternative for the sustainability of the agricultural growth which validates the classical theory that stated that private investment is the engine of growth compared to increases in public expenditures and foreign direct investment and increase in public expenditures and decrease in foreign direct investment. Based on the findings of this study, the following recommendations are made:

i. Given that public expenditures and foreign direct investment significantly affect the growth of the agricultural sector, investment on agricultural targeted programmes should be set up to sustain the growth of the agricultural sector in Cameroon.

ii. Since foreign direct investment is the engine for agricultural growth in Cameroon, incentives such as reduction of tax should be given to attract more foreign investors into the country.
iii. Investment on infrastructure such as roads, railways and dam should be done in order to provide adequate environment to foreigners to invest in the agricultural sector.

References

Abit, M. O. (2014). Export- Income, Economic Growth and Poverty Reduction in Cameroon. *Clarion University of Pennsylvania, Clarion, Pennsylvania, 16*(7), 53–78.

Ahmed, U. J., & Mubarak, U. J. (2014). Significance of Government Social Infrastructure Expenditure on Economic Growth in Nigeria: 1961–2012. *Yobe Journal of Economics, 1*(1), 38–48.

Baye, M. F. (2010). *Exact Configuration of Poverty, Inequality and Polarization Trends in the Distribution of Well-Being in Cameroon* (AERC Research Paper 207, pp. 1–71). African Economic Research Consortium, Nairobi-Kenya.

Belinga, T., Zhou, J., & Guohi, H. (2017). Government Expenditure on Rural Development and Economic Growth in Cameroon. *International Journal of Innovation and Economic Development, 3*(1), 115–122.

Benjamin, N. C., & Devarajan, S. (1986). Oil Revenues and the Cameroonian Economy. In M. G. Schatzberg & I. William Zartman (Eds.), *The Political Economy of Cameroon* (pp. 23–24). New York: Praeger.

CPB Netherlands Bureau for Economic Policy Analysis. (2004, August). *Reducing the Administrative Burden in the European Union* (pp. 65–78).

Delancy, M. W., & Delancy, M. D. (2000). *Historical Dictionary of the Republic of Cameroon* (3rd ed., 400 pp.). Lanham, MD: The Scarecrow Press.

Dissou, Y., & Didic, S. (2011). *Public Infrastructure and Economic Growth* (Working Paper, 80 pp.). Department of Economics, University of Ottawa.

Economic Outlook. (2014). *A Review on the Cameroonian Economy*. www.economicoutlook.org. Accessed on 15 May 2016.

Efiong, A. (2013). Exploring Foreign Direct Investments in Developing African Countries: Their Effects on the Economic Growth in Cameroon (2006–2011). *Scientific Research, 5,* 18–35.

Elijah, U. (2011). An Examination of Public Expenditure, Private Investment and Agricultural Sector Growth in Nigeria: Bounds Testing Approach. *International Journal of Business and Social Science, 2*(13), 79–89.

Essama-Nssah, B., & Bassolé, L. (2010). *A Counterfactual Analysis of the Poverty Impact of Economic Growth in Cameroon* (Policy Research Working Paper 5249, pp. 1–57).

Estache, A., Perrault, J. F., & Savard, L. (2009). *Impact of Infrastructure Spending in Mali: ACGE Modeling Approach* (ECARES Working Papers: 2009_009). Université Libre de Bruxelles, Ecares.

Fambon, S. (2013). *Foreign Capital Inflow and Economic Growth in Cameroon* (Wider Working Paper No. 124, pp. 1–22).

Fambon, S., McKay, A., Timnou, J.P., Kouakep, O. S., Dzossa, A., and Tchakoute, R. (2014). *Growth, Poverty, and Inequality: The Case Study of Cameroon* (UNU-WIDER Working Paper 2014/154, pp. 1–53).

Fan, S. (2007). Case Study #9-1 of the Program, Linkages Between Government Spending, Growth, and Poverty in Uganda and Tanzania. *Food Policy for Developing Countries: The Role of Government in the Global Food System* (pp. 1–15).

Fan, S., Hazell, P., & Thorat, S. (2000). Government Spending, Agricultural Growth and Poverty in India. *American Journal of Agricultural Economics, 82*(4), 1038–1051.

Fatima, G. (2012). Joint Impact of Investment (Public and Private) on the Economic Growth of Pakistan: (Co-Integration Approach). *International Journal of Humanities and Social Science, 2*(15), 171–176.

Forgha, N. G. (2008). Foreign Direct Investment and Economic Performance in Cameroon. *International Review of Business Research Papers, 5*(1), 55–69.

Foueka, R. (2011). *Attempt to Justify the Growth of Public Expenditure in Cameroon*. http://econpapers.reperc.org/paper/pramprapa/40822.htm.

Galal, A. (2003). *Social Expenditure and the Poor in Egypt* (The Egyptian Center for Economic Studies Working Paper No. 89).

Gelauff, G., & Lejour, A. (2006). *Five Lisbon Highlights, the Economic Impact of Reaching These Targets*. CPB.

Ghali, K. H. (1998). Public Investment and Private Capital Formation in a Vector Error Correction Model of Growth. *Applied Economics, 30,* 1–13.

Ibrahim, M. H. (2000). Public and Private Capital Formation and Economic Growth in Malaysia, 1961–1995. *IIUM Journal of Economics and Management, 8*(1), 21–40.

International Fund for Agricultural Development (IFAD). (2012). *Country Strategic Opportunities Programme*. Retrieved from: https://www.ifad.org/en/web/operations/country/id/cameroon.

Jhingan, M. L. (2010). *Macroeconomics Theory* (784 pp.). Delhi, India: Vrinda Publications Pvt Ltd.

Kum, E. B. (2009). *A Study on Foreign Direct Investment in Cameroon* (76 pp.). Thesis submitted to KDI School of Public Policy and Management in

Partial fulfillment of the Requirements for the Degree of Master of Business Administration.

National Institute of Statistics (NIS). (2009). *2nd Survey on the Monitoring of Public Expenditures and the Level of Receipts Satisfaction in the Education and Health* (2nd Budget Tracking [PETSII], pp. 1–119).

Rioja, F. K. (2001). Growth, Welfare, and Public Infrastructure: A General Equilibrium Analysis of Latin American Economies. *Journal of Economic Development, 26*(2), 119–130.

Som, J. (2013). *Women's Role in Cameroon Fishing Communities*. www.fao.org. Retrieved on 21 November 2015.

Sukhdev, P., Kaavya, V., Bassi, A. M., Allen, E., & Mumbunan, S. (2015). *Indonesia Green Economy Model (I-Gem)* (pp. 1–300). Final Report, Low Emission Capacity Building Programme.

Tabi, A. J., Angyie, P. E., & Akwi, T. (2009). Who Benefits from Combined Tax and Public Expenditures Policies in Cameroon? *Journal of Developing Areas, 43,* 1–47.

Tchouassi, G. (2014). Private Capital and Investment Climate for Economic Growth: Empirical Lessons Based on ARDL Bound Test Technique. *European Journal of Sustainable Development, 3*(2), 17–32.

Uboh, E., Oduh, M., & Ujah, O. (2012). *Drivers and Sustainability of Agricultural Growth in Nigeria* (Research Paper 8, pp. 1–51). Published by: African Institute for Applied Economics 54 Nza Sreet, Independence Layout P.O. Box 2147 Enugu, Nigeria.

Van de Walle, D. (1996). *Infrastructure and Poverty in Vietnam* (LSMS Study Working Paper No. 121). Washington, DC: World Bank.

Vaqar, A., Ahsan, A., & Sofia, A. (2013). *Public Infrastructure and Economic Growth in Pakistan: A Dynamic CGE-Micro Simulation Analysis* (Working Paper 2013-01). Partnerships for Economic Policy.

Vedder, R. K., & Gallaway, L. E. (1998). *Government Size and Economic Growth*. Ohio: Washington, DC.

Wautabouna, O. (2012). Public Expenditure Contribution to Pro-Poor Growth in Cote d'Ivoire: A Micro Simulated General Equilibrium Approach. *Modern Economy, 3,* 330–337.

Władysław, W. (2010). Long-Term Simulation Model for a Knowledge-Based Economy. *Argumenta Oeconomica, 2*(25), 1–20.

World Bank. (2013). *Basic Agricultural Public Expenditure Diagnostic Review (2003–12) Republic of Cameroon*. Strengthening National Comprehensive Agricultural Public Expenditure in Sub-Saharan Africa (pp. 1–131).

World factsbook. (2010). *Cameroon Economy*. www.cia.gov/cia/publication/factsbook/goes/htm. Retrieved on 10 November 2015.

CHAPTER 11

Impact of Knowledge Management and Digital Libraries on Climate Change in West and Central Africa

Oluwayemi IbukunOluwa Olatoye, Ndakasharwa Muchaonyerwa, and Tolulope Ayodeji Olatoye

Introduction

Rapid advancements in information and communication technologies within the last three decades have empowered knowledge management and digital libraries in the provision of innovative information resources and services (Oguz 2016). Digital libraries (DLs) promote the expansion of services to libraries, develop existing user services, thereby transforming information delivery through improved and revolutionized means of accessing, creating, utilizing, discovering and managing knowledge across

O. I. Olatoye (✉) · N. Muchaonyerwa
Department of Library and Information Science, University of Fort Hare, Alice, South Africa
e-mail: oolatoye@ufh.ac.za

T. A. Olatoye
Department of Geography and Environmental Science, University of Fort Hare, Alice, South Africa

G. Odularu (ed.), *Nutrition, Sustainable Agriculture and Climate Change in Africa*,
https://doi.org/10.1007/978-3-030-47875-9_11

disciplines irrespective of temporal and geographical barriers. Lesk defines a DL as a collection of organized information in digital format (Khan et al. 2014). Traditionally, it has been the task of libraries to act as the main centres for collecting, making accessible and distributing information in the form of documents (Chowdhury 2010). At each level of our educational system, the library is an invaluable resources centre, as well as being the storehouse of information and its unparalleled importance to educational development (Laltlanmawii 2011). Commonly referred to as the "heart" of the school system and its book collection, digital libraries serve as one of the pillars of the whole structure of education (Säljö 2010). The role of library is two-fold- educational and recreational. A wide range of reading/studying is required for any course, research or discipline if academic excellence is to be achieved. The information, whether in raw form of empirical data or in the highly processed form we call "knowledge" is regarded as very essential to academic pursuit. (Wallace and Van Fleet 2012).

Library services/facilities are custodians and dispensers of recorded knowledge in every form. Furthermore, digital libraries must be adequately equipped, organized, financed and interconnected and their resources are to be available to all people.

Climate is conceptualized as the normal weather condition of an area measured over protracted period of time, generally over 30 years (Olatoye et al. 2019). The concept may be defined additionally as an obvious alteration (increase) in the mean temperature of the atmosphere, landmasses and oceans and is commonly denoted to as "Global Warming" (Badejo et al. 2009). Global climate change has raised global apprehension worldwide on account of its danger to mankind. In the twentieth century, the mean temperature of the earth's surface increased by over 0.5^0 and, according to recent Intergovernmental Panel of Climate Change (IPCC) forecasts, carbon dioxide could rise from about 1.4 to 5.8 °C above the 1990 average by the year 2100. In view of this alarming statistical realities and projections, this paper evaluates the impact of knowledge management on climate change: roles of digital libraries.

Climate experts believe that these evident changes indicated above are caused by the escalating levels of heat-trapping gases known as greenhouse gases in the atmosphere. The presence of these gases in the atmosphere is natural; however, since the commencement of the industrial revolution, their increased concentration in the atmosphere is due essentially to human activities (Olatoye et al. 2019). From the foregoing, it is clear that climate change is already here with us, and is evident by the observable changes like increased earth surface temperature, rise in sea levels, culminating into increased erosion and flooding, as well as the melting of polarized ice caps. Other impacts include widespread storms and alterations in rainfall patterns. These changes have far-reaching consequences, and they impact directly or indirectly on national and household livelihoods and economies.

The past decades have seen extensive research on knowledge and knowledge management (Ma et al. 2010). From the foregoing, the application of Knowledge Management (KM) in this paper involves capturing of knowledge, wisdom and added value experiences of professionals in order to ameliorate the negative consequences of climate change. Also, Dalkir (2013) defined KM as an array of processes geared towards the transfer of intellectual assets to value. Firestone and McElroy (2012), epitomized KM as the process of wealth generation from knowledge or intellectual-based assets. Jennex (2015) opined KM as a methodical process for the acquisition, sustenance, application, sharing, organization and renewal of both explicit and tacit knowledge aimed at the enhancement of performance and value creation. Fernandez and Sabherwal (2010) epitomized KM as efficient and cautious efforts aimed at cultivating, expanding and application of accessible knowledge for purposes of adding value and positive results to an entity so as to accomplish set objectives and fulfil purpose. KM plays a very significant role in librarianship (Hobohm 2011; Kim and Abbas 2010) particularly in the management of recorded or codified knowledge (Kebede 2010), improving the quality of the service as well as in the establishment and preservation of a learning culture (Sakarkar 2014).

The Problem Statement

Increasing CO_2 concentrations in the atmosphere escalate the rate of photosynthesis (Lindner et al. 2010). Other climate change effects include changes in the chemical atmospheric environment, and these have negative impacts on tree growth. Furthermore, concentrations of ozone exacerbate drought stress in trees and diminishes tree biomass (Pecl et al. 2017). Forests are chiefly sensitive to the effects of climate change, due to the fact that the long life-span of trees does not permit for rapid adaptation to environmental alterations.

Climate change is also principally significant as regards precipitation changes, due to the fact that extreme events such as protracted droughts have much more far-reaching consequences on tree growth and survival than gradual changes in average climate conditions. Furthermore, changes in climate will also have concomitant consequences for biotic (incidence and consequences of pest and disease occurrences) and abiotic disturbances (alterations in fire occurrence, as well as alterations regarding wind storm intensity and frequency) with significant implications for ecological systems.

Additionally, climate change strongly affects the population dynamics and incidence of exothermic organisms, such as insect herbivores, as well as the pathogenicity of fungal diseases will be strongly influenced by altered environmental conditions. These different impact factors will affect ecological systems in particular and ultimately, mankind in general. Furthermore, while many studies have considered potential impacts of climate change, less attention has been given to the roles of knowledge management and digital libraries in advocating for mitigating and adaptive capacity to climate change through the generation, processing and delivery of climate change data and information, as well as disseminating information regarding future research in combating climate change.

The Study Rationale

It has been observed in literature (such as Cervone 2011) that there is a gap in the role of digital library project management and KM in climate change related studies. Hence, it is expedient to promote the significance of digital libraries and knowledge-sharing culture on climate change research through institutional learning, change management, strategic partnerships, adoption of best environmental practices, and use of appropriate technologies of knowledge sharing. The development of KM offers new possibilities for developing frontiers of knowledge on climate change (Hočevar and Istenič 2014), as research is required for the utilization of KM in assessing, analysing and forecasting the effects of climate change. Hence, this paper accentuates the impact of knowledge management on climate change, role of digital libraries, as DLs serve as reliable, highly trusted and efficient institutions of consolidating, managing, collecting and processing information records. On the other hand, the academia conducts scientific evaluations, appraisals and predictions of the problems related to climate change. In addition, this paper provides a platform of unifying the roles of DLs and the management of knowledge as sources of information, mitigation, control, as well as adaptation to the environmental challenges of climate change.

This study significantly contributes to science in several ways such as the supply of knowledge regarding explanations, forecasts and adaptive measures to climate change issues. Also, this study promotes the conceptualization, causes and consequences of climate change, as well as ensuring the provision and management of knowledge geared towards integrating climate change studies in biophysical and socio-economic context at multiple scales. Additionally, this study offers scientific and academic information to the general public and policy makers so as to provide guidance in their policy-making decisions. Further, research contributions in this study foster a promising future for librarians, knowledge management experts, as well as academic, socio-economic and environmental policy development through the incorporation of dynamic feedbacks between changing environmental conditions on account of climate change. Also, climate change studies enhance the assessment of complex spatio-environmental interactions, causes and responses in order to better project future trends of anthropogenic activities on the environment. Hence, this study provides valuable scientific information as changes in climatic conditions are more rapidly affecting the livelihoods of societies. Thus, the management of knowledge and the roles of digital libraries in this regard is germane in taking corrective actions in combatting climate change.

The Effects of Climate Change

Climate change is a deviation from the normal climatic condition of an area due to land, atmosphere, ocean and ocean-tropospheric interactions which cause modifications in the balance of gases in the atmosphere, otherwise referred to as radiative forcing factors responsible for global warming and climate change (Milfont 2012). The effects of climate change include increased surface temperature of the earth (Gilman et al. 2010), sea level rise and more flooding: Tide gauge data have shown a global have a global average sea level rise of between 0.1 and 0.2 meters during the twentieth century. By the end of the twenty-first century, sea level rise might hit 0.59 meters (Ellison 2015), and heat waves and periods of rainfall are very likely to become more preponderant (Pramanik et al. 2015). Also, satellite data have shown a probable decrease in snow cover and ice extent by 10% since the late 1960s, and ground-based observations show that there is proof that there has been reduction in the annual duration of lake and river-ice over in the mid and high latitudes of the northern hemisphere, over the twentieth century. During the same period, widespread retreat in mountain glaciers in non-polar regions was also experienced (Derksen and Brown 2012). Similarly, northern hemisphere spring and summer sea-ice extent has decreased by about 10–15% since the 1950s (Andersen and Marshall Shepherd 2013; Olatoye and Odularu 2014; Smedsrud et al. 2017). Screen and Simmonds (2010) and Vihma (2014) also opined that there has been over 40% decline in the thickness of arctic sea-ice during summer to early autumn periods in recent years and a noticeably slow decline in winter sea-ice thickness. Further, Woods and Caballero (2016) stated that increases in drought occurrence and intensity are experienced in several parts of Africa and Asia, and the Sahara Desert is fast encroaching southwards, transforming most of the semi-arid areas of the savannah and grassland regions into desert lands (Geist 2017).

Libraries as Harbingers of Information on Climate Change

Libraries serve as highly trusted and effective institutions to organize, manage and store collections of information (Moran and Morner 2017). Librarians and information experts serve as gateways to access these collections, services and resources supporting them. It is on this premise that transnational research agendas, policies and programmes associated with global climate change provide funding and research support for libraries and librarians geared towards the identification, management, storage, and dissemination of current data and presentation of information in new communication formats and channels. For example, DLs and librarians have played central roles in the development of metadata, data standards directories and developed web pages (as well as their search abilities, menu-driven interfaces), and enhanced accessibility to data and information resources through the World Wide Web and Internet. DLs have also spearheaded data and information management activities to improve identification of, accessibility to, and sharing of data and information in print and electronic formats. Conversely, new opportunities also come with new challenges to change. These barriers represent limitations to express our scientific conceptualization of complex phenomenon (such as climate change), inadequacies in (and access to) the technologies needed to obtain and organize scientific and policy data and information, and our ability to effectively and efficiently share data and information in an equitable manner. International global change research programmes provide libraries and librarian's new roles and responsibilities to facilitate the sharing of data and information resources across disciplines, lines of work and personal agendas. Ready and reliable information accessibility is increasing in significance as a fundamental part of the environmental decision-making process (Gregory et al. 2012). Also, it is germane to state that KM, DLs and other institutions of learning are saddled with important roles regarding the provision of relevant information on climate change concerns pertaining to regulatory requirements, research results, policy initiatives, and increased public orientation and awareness on global climate change concerns have a significant impact on constituent groups such as project administrators, business front-runners, research scientists, policy formulators, programme coordinators, public officers, educationists, students, and the concerned members of the public require efficient, reliable, effective and equitable access to information to sufficiently tackle climate change issues (Olatoye et al. 2019). They also require their need for new data and information products, new publications and documents, new reference and referral services and new data and information delivery services is a challenge for today's digital librarians and information professionals. Librarian developing and providing such services and programmes for this multidisciplinary audience are building bridges to facilitate information, communication and education gaps between constituent groups and foster a greater cross-disciplinary exchange of information, resources (materials and expertise) and ideas. Today's librarians find themselves in roles far removed from the traditional roles as cataloguers, indexers and collection caretakers. Their skills are needed to collaborate with researchers, policy makers, educators, administrators and executive as they evaluate software for data and information management to effectively manage profiles of information products, research projects, business plans, oversee the production of reports, reference books, Web sites and other information tools, to provide training in the use of manual- and online data and information systems, as well as develop marketing strategies for the effective delivery of products and services.

Roles of Selected West African International Organizations on the Control of Climate Change

This study also considers the importance of epitomizing the contributions of selected West African institutions in ameliorating climate change, and these selected organizations include Forum for Agricultural Research in Africa (FARA), International Centre for Research in Agroforestry (ICRAF), Forestry Research Institute of Nigeria (FRIN), Forestry Research Institute of Ghana.

Forum for Agricultural Research in Africa (FARA)

The Forum for Agricultural Research in Africa (FARA) is an apex organization bringing together and forming coalitions of major stakeholders in agricultural research and development in the region. It is a strategic platform that fosters continental and global networking to reinforce the capacities of Africa's agricultural science and innovation community from research, education/training, extension and civil society engaged in agriculture. Established in 2001, the Forum encompasses all stakeholders, African and non-African, who are committed to enabling African agricultural development and the achievement of the Millennium Development Goal on climate change and environmental stability. Some of the major achievements of FARA in combatting climate change are listed below.

The Development of strategic partnerships to combat climate change: As part of the Development Smart Innovation through Research in Agriculture (DeSIRA), the European Commission (EC) and International Fund for Agricultural Development (IFAD) are jointly supporting the Comprehensive Africa Agriculture Development Programme (CAADP) ex-pillar IV Organisations in implementing a science-led and climate relevant agricultural programme; Supporting Implementation of a Science-Led and Climate-Relevant Agricultural Transformation in Africa (SISTA). The Forum for Agricultural Research in Africa (FARA) and partner sub-regional agricultural research organizations are benefiting from the programme, which seeks among other things to contribute to combat climate change and its impacts (SDG 13) among others. With financing from the European Union, FARA is implementing individual projects as part of the overall programme with overall objective to enable agricultural research and innovation, including extension services, to contribute effectively to food and nutrition security, to economic development and climate mitigation in Africa. This will be achieved by improving the capacity, effectiveness and positioning of the regional and sub-regional agriculture research and extension organizations as well as National Agriculture Research Systems, and by promoting collaboration and knowledge sharing among the organizations.

The International Centre for Research In Agroforestry (ICRAF)

The International Centre for Research in Agroforestry, ICRAF, has an ultimate purpose guiding its research. It is to work towards mitigating tropical deforestation, land depletion and rural poverty through improved agroforestry systems. Its goal is to initiate and assist in the generation and dissemination of appropriate agroforestry technologies for resource-poor farmers and other land users. Some of the major achievements of ICRAF in combatting climate change are listed below.

Restoration of Degraded Land for Food Security: The goal of the project is to reduce food insecurity and improve livelihoods of poor people living in African drylands by restoring degraded land, and returning it to effective and sustainable tree, crop and livestock production, thereby increasing land profitability and landscape and livelihood resilience.

The Drylands Development Programme (DRYDEV) is a six-year initiative (August 2013–July 2019) funded by the Ministry of Foreign Affairs (MoFA) of the Netherlands, with a significant financial contribution from World Vision Australia (WVA). The World Agroforestry Centre (ICRAF) is the overall implementing agency. DRYDEV is designed to provide relevant and contextually appropriate support to smallholder farmers in selected dryland areas of Burkina Faso, Mali, Niger, Ethiopia, among others.

The Programme Building Resilience and Adaptation to Climate Extremes and Disasters (BRACED), aims to improve the integration of disaster risk reduction and climate adaptation methods into development approaches. BRACED is implemented by 15 consortia to build the resilience of sedentary and nomadic populations in 13 countries across Africa, South and South-East Asia. The project aiming at improving community resilience through climate smart agriculture, health and early warning systems is implemented in Chad and Sudan.

Forestry Research Institute of Nigeria (FRIN)

FRIN is the only research institute in Nigeria with mandate into sustainable forest management, forest product development & utilization, forest conservation & protection, forest economics & extension, environmental modelling as well as the management and wildlife and tourism. Some of the major achievements of FRIN in combatting climate change are listed below.

The development of a successfully implemented green economy model for communities around biodiversity conserved environment (land mass) which has now been adopted by UNESCO for the region; The coordination of the ongoing National Afforestation programme under the Green Bond concept of this Administration whereby over 500 hectares of indigenous tree species had been planted; Successful Enactment of An Act to Establish the Forestry Research Institute of Nigeria for Forestry Research, Education And Training In Nigeria; and For Related Matters; Successful reduction of the gestation period of seven indigenous economic tree species from about 15–25 years to 5–7 years; Reclaimed and secured all encroached land and resources of the Institute; Reconstituted and equipped the Biotechnology Centre of the Institute for Mass propagation of seedlings to meet the National Afforestation programme requirement; Initiated and completed the documentation of two additional UNESCO adopted Biosphere Reserves and one National Transboundary Biosphere Reserve. This is quite notable, because prior to this time, Nigeria had only one of such UNESCO Biosphere Reserves which was established far back in 1977, over four decades ago; Established the Patency and Enterprise incubation Centre for the Institute that has added value and currently offers about fifteen (15) forest and medicinal products; Established the largest conservation Arboretum in West Africa for the conservation of rare, threatened and endangered tree species, wildlife and bird sanctuary measuring fifteen (15) hectares; Established a two hectare herbal garden for the recently created Biomedicinal Research Centre of the Institute; Established six strategic Rural Resource Centres for communities' engagement, capacity building and extension services.

Forestry Research Institute of Ghana (FORIG)

Forestry Research Institute of Ghana is a centre of excellence in forestry research in the humid tropics, saddled with demand-driven research, capacity building and promotion of technologies for sustainable management of forest resources for the benefit of society. The institute also conducts high quality user-focused forestry research that generates scientific knowledge and appropriate technologies, disseminate forestry-related information for the improvement of the social, economic and environmental well-being as well as enhancing sustainable development, conservation and efficient utilization of Ghana's forest resources. Some of the major achievements of FORIG in combatting climate change are listed below.

Savannah Forest Boundary Transition in West Africa—coupling the energy balance and hydrology and carbon cycles across the biome zot: This research aims at investigating vegetation interaction with soil, climate and edaphic factors in a forest savannah-ecotone in West Africa, to elucidate the dynamics of vegetation change in the light of fire mediated feedbacks and alternate states of forest and savannah. The study is being conducted in the Kogyae Strict Nature Reserve in Ghana.

Carbon Use Efficiency in the conservation of tropical forests: The project addresses the relative importance of photosynthesis and autotrophic respiration in determining forest function in intact and disturbed tropical African forests. From the foregoing, comprehensive carbon cycle assessment plots have been established and replicated across two contrasting countries in Africa, namely Ghana (West Africa) and Gabon (Central Africa). In Ghana, the project is implemented in different ecological zones namely: the Bobiri Forest Reserve (moist semi-deciduous zone), Ankasa Forest Reserve (wet evergreen zone) and the Kogyae Strict Nature Reserve (dry semi-deciduous zone).

Advancing REDD+ in Ghana: Preparation of REDD+ Pilot Schemes in Off-Reserve Forests and Agroforests: This research is aimed at developing a framework to guide the implementation of REDD+ from the national to the local level. This will allow Ghana to take stock of existing initiatives that have the potential to be considered under REDD+ , as well as to concretely analyse promising REDD+ activities.

The objective is to provide Ghana with proposals for the enhancement of sustainable off-reserve production systems under REDD+ schemes with a focus on local livelihood improvement. Some of the outputs of this project include a draft guide on the implementation of REDD+ in Ghana: criteria and modalities for developing a REDD+ project together with a policy brief defining the governance structure of carbon assets.

Rehabilitation of Degraded Forests for Sustainable WoodFuel Production and Climate Change Mitigation in the Forest-Savannah Transition Zone of Ghana.

This project contributes to ameliorating the effects of climate change and ensures sustained socio-economic development of forest-dependent communities and reduction in forest degradation in the forest savannah transition zone of Ghana through the promotion of smallholder and commercial tree plantations that could ensure sustainability of the resource base. Baseline surveys have been completed with the identification of six communities where test plots for planting wood fuel would be sited. Some species both indigenous and exotic have also been selected for planting on the plots.

Characterization and efficient utilization of emerging wood fuel species for charcoal production in the savannah transition zone of Ghana: This research mainly identifies and characterizes wood fuel species and assess their availability, extent of extraction and utilization in the forest savannah transition zone of Ghana. The ultimate aim is to assist in suggesting further research and development interventions for ensuring sustainable utilization and management of wood fuel resources.

National Forest Plantation Development Programme: The assessment was aimed at ascertaining total area established, seedling survival rates, general condition of forest plantations health and safety standards for the workforce and other relevant activities towards meeting the overall objectives. Further, this project aims at restoring the degraded forest cover of Ghana, improve environmental quality and provide an avenue for west Africans to tap benefits from emerging climate change markets for carbon sequestration, reduction of wood deficit situation as well as the enhancement of food crop production to ensure food security.

Conclusion

Climate change phenomenon is of major concern to the sustainability of the earth, ecological systems and future human welfare in general. Climate change culminates into numerous potential problems such as reduced rainfall, flooding, reduction in vegetal productivity, environmental degradation, etc. From the foregoing, the following recommendations are proffered in order to curtail the negative consequences of climate change.

There is need to raise awareness, orientate and sensitize the general public on the warning signs and effects of climate change. Such information should be disseminated to the grassroots. A clear understanding of climate change is imperative for encouraging and implementing appropriate adaptations. Information needs to be disseminated regarding:

- The nature of climate change and its potential to cause problems in all aspects of human life;
- The potential short and long term impacts of climate change;
- The climate change adaptation options available to man. This can be actualized through the electronic and print media, by NGOs, federal and local governments, International Organizations, CBOs and the academia at large. Other strategic measures include national campaigns, public outreach programmes, presentations and stakeholder initiatives and workshops on climate change issues.

There is need for the nonstop provision of cutting-edge sustainable development policies, programmes and research that would stimulate environmental safety concerns and security. Examples of these include the adoption of sustainable agricultural practices, forest conservation, reduction in emissions of carbon, afforestation, reforestation, carbon sequestration, sustainable harvesting methods, agroforestry, and sustainable utilization of wood fuels, just to mention a few.

- Mitigation and Adaptation Strategies: These are two methods that are germane in tackling climate change. Mitigation strategies are activities geared towards confronting climate change causes, such as the reduction in emissions of greenhouse gases, while adaptation strategies are actions that diminish the effects of actual and expected changes in the climate, such as the reinforcement and consolidation of traditional coping mechanisms.
- Increasing Scientific Capacity: These include strategies such as the enhancement of scientific capacity by improving access to climate data, development of modelling capabilities and having proper mechanisms in place to disseminate and process data for the general public, so as to promote sensitization of potential climate change impacts. It also equips societies with necessary climate information which are essential for national impact assessments, adaptation and

sustainable development planning, hence, increasing their adaptation capacities.

- Information networking: This should be fostered by government (at all levels of administration), libraries, NGOs, media, academia as well as environmental information outfits. Such synergy will be boosted through the creation of National Information parastatals on climate change. This parastatals will be saddled with generating, collating, storing, evaluating and supplying information as well as formulating policies on climate change control, environmental conservation and management. It is also recommended that national policies on environmental protection be regularly reviewed to incorporate mitigation and adaptive measures that would battle climate change challenges.

References

Andersen, T. K., & Marshall Shepherd, J. (2013). Floods in a Changing Climate. *Geography Compass, 7*(2), 95–115.

Badejo, S. O. O., Akintola, B. A., Olatoye, T. A., & Pelemo, O. J. (2009, June 9–11). Building Nigeria's Capacity to Adapt to the Effects of Climate Change. In *Being a Paper Published in the Conference Proceedings of the 2nd Annual Conference of the Institute of Ecology & Environmental Studies*. Ile-Ife, Nigeria: Obafemi Awolowo University.

Cervone, H. F. (2011). Overcoming Resistance to Change in Digital Library Projects. *OCLC Systems & Services: International Digital Library Perspectives*.

Chowdhury, G. G. (2010). *Introduction to Modern Information Retrieval*. Facet publishing.

Dalkir, K. (2013). *Knowledge Management in Theory and Practice*. London: Routledge.

Derksen, C., & Brown, R. (2012). Spring Snow Cover Extent Reductions in the 2008–2012 Period Exceeding Climate Model Projections. *Geophysical Research Letters, 39*(19), 1–6.

Ellison, J. C. (2015). Vulnerability Assessment of Mangroves to Climate Change and Sea-level Rise Impacts. *Wetlands Ecology and Management, 23*(2), 115–137.

Fernandez, I. B., & Sabherwal, R. (2010). *Knowledge Management Systems and Processes*. Armonk and London: ME Sharpe.

Firestone, J. M., & McElroy, M. W. (2012). *Key Issues in the New Knowledge Management*. London: Routledge.

Geist, H. (2017). *The Causes and Progression of Desertification*. London: Routledge.

Gilman, S. E., Urban, M. C., Tewksbury, J., Gilchrist, G. W., & Holt, R. D. (2010). A Framework for Community Interactions Under Climate Change. *Trends in Ecology & Evolution, 25*(6), 325–331.

Gregory, R., Failing, L., Harstone, M., Long, G., McDaniels, T., & Ohlson, D. (2012). *Structured Decision Making: A Practical Guide to Environmental Management Choices*. New York: Wiley.

Hobohm, H. C. (Ed.). (2011). *Knowledge Management: Libraries and Librarians Taking Up the Challenge* (Vol. 108). Berlin: Walter de Gruyter.

Hočevar, D. K., & Istenič, M. Č. (2014). In Pursuit of Knowledge-based Slovenia: Is Knowledge Transfer to Agriculture Stuck in Faculties? *Anthropological Notebooks, 20*(3).

Jennex, M. E. (2015). Knowledge Management. *Wiley Encyclopedia of Management* (pp. 1–6).

Kebede, G. (2010). Knowledge Management: An Information Science Perspective. *International Journal of Information Management, 30*(5), 416–424.

Khan, A., Ahmed, S., & Masrek, M. N. (2014). Scholars' Satisfaction with Digital Library Collection and Gaps in the Provision of Effective Information Resources and Services: A Pakistani Perspective. *Journal of Electronic Resources Librarianship, 26*(4), 250–267.

Khan, H. U., Artail, H. A., Malik, Z., & Niazi, M. (2014, August). Information Technology Adoption, Possible Challenges, and Framework of Supply Chain Management: A Case Study of a Leading Gulf Economy. In *2014 4th International Conference on Engineering Technology and Technopreneuship (ICE2T)* (pp. 1–5). IEEE.

Kim, Y. M., & Abbas, J. (2010). Adoption of Library 2.0 Functionalities by Academic Libraries and Users: A Knowledge Management Perspective. *The Journal of Academic Librarianship, 36*(3), 211–218.

Laltlanmawii, R. (2011). *An Evaluation of Use of E-Resources In*. Guwahati: Indian Institute of Technology Library.

Lindner, M., Maroschek, M., Netherer, S., Kremer, A., Barbati, A., Garcia-Gonzalo, J. et al. (2010). Climate Change Impacts, Adaptive Capacity, and Vulnerability of European Forest Ecosystems. *Forest Ecology and Management, 259*(4), 698–709.

Ma, W., Fang, J., Yang, Y., & Mohammat, A. (2010). Biomass Carbon Stocks and their Changes in Northern China's Grasslands During 1982–2006. *Science China Life Sciences, 53*(7), 841–850.

Milfont, T. L. (2012). The Interplay Between Knowledge, Perceived Efficacy, and Concern about Global Warming and Climate Change: A One-Year Longitudinal Study. *Risk Analysis: An International Journal, 32*(6), 1003–1020.

Moran, B. B., & Morner, C. J. (2017). *Library and Information Center Management*. Santa Barbara: ABC-CLIO.

Oguz, A., & Ataseven, N. (2016). Relationship Between the Lifelong Learning Tendency and Information Literacy Self-efficacy of Students. *The Anthropologist, 24*(1), 28–34.

Olatoye, T. A., Bada, S. O., Akintola, B. A., Pelemo, O. J., Ogoliegbune, O. M., & Sowunmi I. L. (2011, December 5–10). Carbon Sequestration Through Reforestation and its Emerging Opportunities in Nigeria. *Being a Paper Published in the 34th Annual Proceeding of Forestry Association of Nigeria [FAN]* (13 pp.). Oshogbo, Osun State.

Olatoye, T. A., Odularu, G. O. A. (2014, October). *Geographical Information Systems Analysis of Landcover Change and Fuel Wood Production in Gambari Forest Reserve*. A Publication in Book of Abstracts at 24th International Union of Forestry Research Organizations (UIFRO). World Congress to be held in Salt Lake City, UT, USA.

Olatoye, T. A., Kalumba, A. M., & Mazinyo, S. P. (2019). Exploratory Review of Urban Expansion, Coastal Vegetation Environments (CVEs) and Sustainability Paradox. *Being a Paper Published in the Journal of Human Ecology, 67*(1–3): 21–30. https://doi.org/10.31901/24566608.2019/67.

Pecl, G. T., Araújo, M. B., Bell, J. D., Blanchard, J., Bonebrake, T. C., Chen, I. C. et al. (2017). Biodiversity Redistribution Under Climate Change: Impacts on Ecosystems and Human Well-Being. *Science, 355*(6332), eaai9214.

Pramanik, M. K., Biswas, S. S., Mukherjee, T., Roy, A. K., Pal, R., & Mondal, B. (2015). Sea level Rise and Coastal Vulnerability Along the Eastern Coast of India Through Geo-Spatial Technologies. *Journal of Remote Sensing & GIS, 4*(2), 1–8.

Sakarkar, D. S. D. (2014). Knowledge Management in Academic Libraries. *Library Science-An International Registered and Referred Monthly Journal*, 134–135.

Säljö, R. (2010). Digital Tools and Challenges to Institutional Traditions of Learning: Technologies, Social Memory and the Performative Nature of Learning. *Journal of Computer Assisted Learning, 26*(1), 53–64.

Screen, J. A., & Simmonds, I. (2010). The Central Role of Diminishing Sea Ice in Recent Arctic Temperature Amplification. *Nature, 464*(7293), 1334–1337.

Smedsrud, L. H., Halvorsen, M. H., Stroeve, J. C., Zhang, R., & Kloster, K. (2017). Fram Strait Sea Ice Export Variability and September Arctic Sea Ice Extent Over the Last 80 Years. *The Cryosphere, 11*(1), 65–79.

Vihma, T. (2014). Effects of Arctic Sea Ice Decline on Weather and Climate: A Review. *Surveys in Geophysics, 35*(5), 1175–1214.

Wallace, D. P., & Van Fleet, C. J. (2012). *Knowledge into Action: Research and Evaluation in Library and Information Science*. ABC-CLIO.

Woods, C., & Caballero, R. (2016). The Role of Moist Intrusions in Winter Arctic Warming and Sea Ice Decline. *Journal of Climate, 29*(12), 4473–4485.

CHAPTER 12

Conclusion: Fostering Nutrition Security, Climate Adaptation and Sustainable Agriculture Strategies Amid COVID-19 Pandemic

Gbadebo Odularu, Olatokunbo Akinseye Aluko, Adenike Odularu, Monica Akokuwebe, and Adebola Adedugbe

G. Odularu (✉)
Department of Economics and Finance, Bay Atlantic University, Washington, DC, USA

O. A. Aluko
Bestfield Business and Management Consultants, Milton Keynes, UK

A. Odularu
Federal Ministry of Industry, Trade & Investment, Garki, Nigeria

M. Akokuwebe
University of Ibadan, Ibadan, Nigeria

A. Adedugbe
Farmideas Nigeria, Abuja, Nigeria

G. Odularu (ed.), *Nutrition, Sustainable Agriculture and Climate Change in Africa*,
https://doi.org/10.1007/978-3-030-47875-9_12

Sustainable Agri-Food Policy Recommendations for Africa

Improved dietary patterns and nutrition security have been identified as major drivers of healthy living. In other words, the provision of tailor-made dietary and nutrition information services is increasingly gaining importance as a vital preventative strategy against selected non-communicative diseases (NCDs). Based on the available literature, there is a positive correlation between improved dietary patterns and better health outcomes on one hand, as well as the use of this evidences to influence health-related policy making processes on the other hand. According to Feeding America, 'Food insecurity describes a household's inability to provide enough food for every person to live an active, healthy life. Food insecurity is one way we can measure and assess the risk of hunger. In the United States currently, 1 in 9 people struggle with hunger'. Its effects include health complications and serious health-care conditions. Nutrition and dietary intake pose profound impact on health throughout the human life course and is inextricably linked with cognitive and social development, especially in early childhood, as well as on diet-related infectious and non-communicable diseases (NCD) in adulthood. In the developed countries, like the U.S., excessive intakes of macro-nutrients (over-nutrition) and sub-optimal intakes of micro-nutrients (hidden hunger), mainly because of low fruit and vegetable consumption, lead to obesity and related NCDs. Further, the diet quality of U.S. children is sub-optimal and according to the Dietary Guidelines for Americans (DGA) children between 9 and 13 years of age should consume at least 4–5 servings of fruits and vegetables (FV) each day, while data reveals that more than 80% of 9–13-year-old children do not consume the minimum recommended daily servings of fruits and vegetables (Arcan et al. 2019). The verifiable estimate is that one in every 5 Sub-Saharan African is undernourished.

As selected African governments continue to provide limited palliative measures in the form of either cash transfer or food items, one of the challenges being faced border on alleged diversion of stimulus packages by government officials, who were saddled with the distribution process. The mechanism put in place by the executive arm of government has been 'hijacked by politicians' who gave out the items to loyal party members at the expense of the very poor in the society. Palliatives from government have not really been effective. The distribution channel has been very poor and ineffective. The items have not reached the poorest of the poor as government envisaged but in hands of party chieftains and faithful. In some instance, the quality of the palliative (raw food, bread, and beverage) has been questioned as the items are rarely enough as a meal for a family of four. The impact of the lockdown is felt across the country through unevenly. Farm operations are the worst hit, while small businesses in the cities are faced with enormous challenges. Governments at all levels must develop a policy framework that will respond to these impacts to avoid supply chain disruptions, higher food prices and serious economic fallout for millions of small business owners. It advised that there are many strategies that can support community resilience and mental health, protect access to essential goods and services, and limit the economic impact of stay-at-home measures where these are deemed necessary.

Climate change is already affecting the livelihoods of smallholder farmers in the West and Central Africa who rely on rain-fed agricultural techniques which may make food shortages more acute as the regions is facing challenges (FAO 2010; IPPC 2001). Farmers in the region are trying to cope with irregular rainfall, flooding, farm destruction by militant groups and degraded soil. With the shift towards Sustainable Development Goals (SDGs) approaches that severe multiple purpose and provide cross-cutting benefits are highly needed in Africa and elsewhere. For example, achieving food security is unmanageable without adaptation and resilience to climate change measures and practices that not only support farmers in producing enough food to meet people's nutritional needs, but that also preserve ecosystems from degradation. Approaches with the potential for informing and guiding policy and practices are imperative. This article examines the influence of climate change variability on food systems among smallholder farmers with the aim of enhancing food systems and resilient livelihoods, and ultimately achieves food security in a changing climate.

The agricultural sector (in the broad sense, including forestry, animal production, aquaculture, etc.) represents the dominant part of the economies in most countries in West and Central Africa and provides the majority of employments and livelihoods (Clover 2003). Agriculture according to most experts, will continue to have a central role to play in the development process of the African continent. As the African population continues to grow, diet changes associated with rising incomes drive greater demand for food and other agricultural products, while global food systems are increasingly threatened by land degradation, climate change and other stressors. Ultimately, climate change is about human acting in socio-ecological settings in which biophysical, socio-cultural, economic, institutional, political and legal mechanism operate. Agriculture must change to meet both rising demand and become ecologically sustainable. Approaches with the potential for informing and guiding policy and practices are imperative. One of these approaches is Ecosystem-based adaptation (EbA), which provides flexible, cost effective and broadly applicable alternatives for building robust food systems on less inputs and reducing the impacts of climate change. Practices such as agro-forestry, buffer strips, on-site water conservation, use of native species, etc. practised by farmers in these two regions have demonstrated that ecological-based approaches can provide just one right framework for catalyzing transformative change on a larger scale.

The infusion of the indigenous knowledge and the scientific views and cross-cutting initiatives at the local and national levels has led to the restoration of both terrestrial and marine/aquatic species. A range of specific techniques were adopted to enhance climate change adaptation, among these Payment for Ecosystem services (PES), preservation and promotion of indigenous species and sustainable harvesting practices, afforestation and mangrove rehabilitation, water system rehabilitation (including reservoirs, wastewater reuse, and early maturing and drought resistant crop adaptation) were among the most successful practices.

As Africa continues to experience population growth, natural systems that support us all may not be able to withstand the pressure that this growth exerts. Water scarcity, land degradation and the loss of natural (ecosystem) services we all depend on, point to fundamental problems caused by unsustainable development. The direct causes of inadequate food access are poverty, environmental stressors and conflict. Catastrophes like floods, earthquakes, drought and conflict in vulnerable countries force the poor to abandon their homes and livelihoods, creating even more victims of hunger. It is in this complex system that disasters emerge, and that society has to cope with. Human and food security within the context of climate change remains relatively under explored. It has now been widely established that the pervasive societal emphasis on the modes and volume of food production in developing countries has been detrimental to resolving problems relating to food distribution, affordability and accessibility. The singular focus on production has consequently amplified food insecurity in many parts of the world. Agriculture must change to meet both rising demand and become ecologically sustainable. Agriculture has significant linkages to poverty and hunger, nutrition and health, peace and security and preserving the world's natural resources. Variability in climatic conditions has been argued to be a stumbling block to food security in most developing countries and especially in Sub-Saharan Africa. This is because, Sub-Saharan Africa already experiences high temperatures and low (and highly variable) precipitation; second, because the economies are highly dependent on agriculture and third, because there is low adoption of modern technology. Extreme poverty, hunger and undernourishment can be eradicated by 2030 while protecting and even reversing harm to natural resources, despite the challenges of climate change and weather extremes.

Further, the search for synergies should intensify as governments at different levels (International, national and local) engage private and citizen groups to identify opportunities for resource optimization through efficient use of nutritional, environmental and budgetary resources. How equipped is the scientific community to capture changes in human behaviour (such as cropping practices), analyze their impact on biophysical processes and build capacity of governments to predict and respond to environmental shocks and stresses (examples: decline in soil fertility and air quality). We must also realize that smallholder farmers play a key role when it comes to ensuring food for all and climate change and hence need our help. A more integrated approach is needed which recognizes the impacts of, and relationship between agriculture and other development activities. By neglecting the management of natural resources, unsustainable pro-poor land and water allocations, which increase resource efficiency, our ability to as a global community to meet future food needs and address climate change in West and Central Africa may be compromised. With the anticipated impacts on coastal ecosystem, from climate change, it is vital that measures be put in place to ensure measures for resilience, to allow a system to absorb and recover from the effects of a hazardous event and maintain its essential functions and structures.

Thus, there is need for increasing amount of innovative research that analyze the determinants of across-the-communities disparities in nutrient intake from dietary sources (not supplements) among vulnerable groups—infants, children, mothers, elderly, etc with a focus on priority nutrients and food groups for future food assistance package revisions for most underserved communities in Africa, and all over the world. In recent times, global health and hunger-relief organizations have continually collaborated in solving seemingly unsolvable community challenges. Understanding the relationship between food, diet, nutrition, health, the environment as well as the multifaceted nature of global health.

According to the Food and Agriculture Organization of the United Nations (FAO), the COVID-19 pandemic is impacting global food systems, disrupting regional agricultural value chains and posing risks to household food security. Most African Governments have been engaging at their respective ministerial level to improve COVID-19 food supply chains. The COVID-19 crisis require a consolidated intervention which places emphasis on sustainable agricultural systems towards addressing issues, challenges and innovative solutions that would permit easy access for the food supply chain on the continent and in alignment with broader government's objective of ensuring a healthy and food secured nation in the face of COVID-19 Pandemic.

There is a dire need for awareness creation, knowledge dissemination and capacity strengthening on enhanced implementation of sustainable agriculture strategies and programmes. Apparently, there are ongoing huge disruptions as well as losses of employment and income opportunities in the informal sector which is the bulk of most African economies for fostering sustainable agriculture practices. In addition, agri-food exports and horticultural supply chains are being disrupted in Eastern and Southern African countries. Consequently, countries and development partners have deployed innovative tools in combating not only the spread of the virus but also the adverse impacts of its rapid evolution on livelihoods and communities all over the world. For instance, the African Development Bank Group has allocated for the financial year 2020 the amount of USD 10 billion in resources for supporting Regional Member Countries (RMC) and their private sector enterprises in response to the COVID-19 outbreak.

In addition to financial resources being allocated to develop vaccines, there is dire need for evidence-based knowledge capacities strengthening and sustainable agricultural programming, as well as technical assistance support to making prompt decisions in addressing COVID-related knowledge gaps and policy guidance to African countries in a post COVID-19 era. For instance, the African Development Institute (ADI) manages its

Virtual Capacity Development Academy (VCDA)[1] Global Community of Practice (G-CoP) to facilitate policy guidance, technical assistance and knowledge support on COVID-19 Response Strategies in Africa.

From an macroeconomic viewpoint, COVID-19 is a sudden shock which poses unprecedented impacts on the global economy but with more devastating implications for the developing world, especially most Sub-Saharan African countries (SSA), which ordinarily and before-COVID-19 were struggling to combat their food and nutrition insecurity, climate change challenges, market infrastructure and logistics deficiencies and public health challenges. Some of the current strategies which are aimed at crushing the COVID-19 trends are border (aviation and land borders) closures, lockdown, social distancing, disruption of national, regional and global food and non-food supply chains, etc. For instance, sudden decline in the global demand for African agricultural exports such as cocoa whose world price dropped by 25% in late April 2020, thereby reducing exports earnings as well as revenue generation capacities at the time when fiscal stimulus is most critically needed. The unsustainable nature of this agri-food systems has resulted in the current responses to the COVID-19 pandemic such that panic buying, exchange volatilities, food supply chain disruptions, protectionist measures and severe children malnutrition are being experienced in most SSA countries. By implication, there is need to develop and implement more resilient and sustainable agri-food programmes in order to build on rather than wipe out some of the Pre-COVID-19 socio-economic gains recorded in African countries, as well as being capable to absorb current and future shocks and related-pandemics.

[1] VCDA is a virtual interactive collaborative environment that enables a consortium of certified global experts and anchor institutions to engage in facilitated policy dialogue and to provide evidence-based policy advice, technical assistance and training to its clients on specialized subject areas.

References

Arcan, C., Friend, S., Flattum, C. F., Story, M., & Fulkerson, J. A. (2019). Fill 'Half Your Child's Plate with Fruits and Vegetables': Correlations with Food-Related Practices and the Home Food Environment. *Appetite, 133*, 77–82. https://doi.org/10.1016/j.appet.2018.10.017.

Clover, J. (2003). Food Security in Sub-Saharan Africa. *African Security Review*, *12*(1), 5–15.

Food and Agricultural Organization. (2010). *Climate Change Implications for Food Security and Natural Resources Management in Africa*. Twenty-Sixth Regional Conferences for Africa.

Intergovernmental Panel on Climate Change. (2001). *Climate Change 2001: Impacts, Adaptation and Vulnerability* (IPCC Working Group 11, Third Assessment Report). McCarthy J. J., Canzaiani, O. F.

Index

G. Odularu (ed.), *Nutrition, Sustainable Agriculture and Climate Change in Africa*,
https://doi.org/10.1007/978-3-030-47875-9

The manufacturer's authorised representative in the EU is Springer Nature Customer Service Centre GmbH, Europaplatz 3, 69115 Heidelberg, Germany. If you have any concerns regarding our products, please contact ProductSafety@springernature.com

Printed and bound by CPI Group (UK) Ltd, Croydon, CR0 4YY
05/10/2026
02228123-0002